# Death Recorded

## CAPITAL PUNISHMENT IN SUFFOLK 1732 - 1900

# Pip Wright

# Death Recorded

Acknowledgements are due to a number of people without whose help,
the publication of this book would not have been possible.
In particular, thanks are due to Adrian Pye, the staff at the Suffolk
Record Offices at Ipswich and Bury St. Edmunds, the Family History
Centre at Norwich and the Public Record Office at Kew.
Special thanks to Diana Whiting for her help in
proof-reading and editing this book

**Other books by Pip Wright:**
*Lydia*

**Books by Pip & Joy Wright**
*The Amazing Story of John H. Steggall, 'The Suffolk Gipsy'*
*Newspapers in Suffolk* **(6 vols.)**
*Grave Reports*
*Witches in and around Suffolk*
*Bygone Cotton*

*Diary of a Poor Suffolk Woodman* **(with Léonie Robinson)**
**pub. by Poppyland Publishing**
**See these all at pipwright.com**

# Up and make ready, ye lovers of fun!

On with your holiday dress and be gay!
Now that the Sheriff has work to be done,
Business with pleasure he mingles today.
Some may go hunting with guns, and a few,
Rods in their hands, little fish may pursue;
Ours is the sport which is sanctioned by law -
We go a-hanging - a-hanging, hurrah!
Two months ago, on a rare drunken bout,
Billy, his comrade, the criminal slew;
Murder's a deed that is vile, without doubt
Ergo, the law will turn murderer too.
As to the place where the liquor he got,
Liquor which maddened him - yonder's the spot,
Sammy who keeps it, approves of the law -
He goes for hanging, for hanging, hurrah!
Bright shines the sun on the place where you see
Yonder, tall gallows, substantial and bare,
Wait a few hours and a fellow will be
Dancing fandangoes of fun in the air.
Gathered in groups at the gallows, behold
Parents and children, maids, wives, young and old
Waiting the time when the halter shall draw -
They go for hanging, for hanging, hurrah!
Pickpockets plenty are - mark how they go,
Slyly and coolly to work at their trade!
Business is business and people must know
Too much attention to that can't be paid.
Swearing and fighting and kicking, the crowd
Utter their blasphemous curses aloud -
Righteous examples are set by the law,
Good comes from hanging - from hanging, hurrah!
Look at the criminal! Please ye, a look!
Standing beside him, the hangman you see,
There is the priest with his gown and his book,
Galloping gaily, they go to the tree.
Thanks to the priest who the hangman befriend,
Choking such knaves as 'twere labour to mend;
Hanging they say is Levitical law -
Cheers for the clergy, they're Christians, hurrah!
Firmly and proudly, the culprit looks round,
Holding his head with a satisfied air,
Murmurs applauding go over the ground -
Down pops the priest with the felon to prayer.

"How interesting his looks are," says Ann,
"Yes," answers Sal, "And he'll die like a man!"
Elegant talk for young maidens, but - pshaw!
Shout for the hanging, the hanging, hurrah!
Prayers are all finished, and now for the fun;
Over his features, the cap has been drawn;
Ketch, and his comrade, the preacher, get down,
Crack goes the whip, and the carriage moves on.
Wonderful sight for the Christian to see,
Merrily dancing on nothing is he;
Though there's no fiddler a hornpipe to saw,
Light are his leaps.  He's hanging, hurrah!
After the rope has been severed in twain,
Home go the people and joyfully sing,
Heaven will receive who the gallows has slain -
Does not the clergyman settle the thing?
Home go the people and talk of it all,
Children in nursery, servants in hall;
Bob hangs the cat in the manner he saw,
Hung at the gallows, God's Image!  Hurrah!
Rouse ye good clergymen, servants of God!
Stand by my side while I fight for your fun;
Hanging preserves us from shedding of blood,
Remedy like it there never was one.
Rally your forces, thump pulpits and be
Clerical guards of the good gallows tree!
What if our Saviour denounces the law?
You go for hanging - for hanging, hurrah!

*Suffolk Chronicle:  January 18th 1845*

# Death Recorded

In March 1780, a ne'er-do-well by the name of **Jonathan Sawyer** was tried at Bury St. Edmunds for burglaries at Cretingham and Brundish. He was found guilty and, along with three Ipswich thieves, was condemned to death. It wasn't difficult to get a death sentence. Any number of crimes carried the death penalty at that time. But it didn't mean that the ultimate price would be paid. The three Ipswich thieves were all reprieved and given the dubious alternative of serving as soldiers in war-torn parts of the world. That was not to be for Jonathan Sawyer. He was carted back to Ipswich gaol, from where he was taken on April 8th to Rushmere Heath for a public hanging.

*Jonathan Sawyer, otherwise Lock, who is to be executed this day for a burglary, has behaved in a very proper manner since his condemnation. He confesses the crime for which he is to suffer, and many others which he has been guilty of, and acknowledges the justice of the punishment inflicted upon him; which he hopes will be a warning to others. He is only 18 years old. An account of his life will be published this day, and may be had of the printers at 1d each. Although he is but a young offender, there are many transactions in this account, well worth the perusal of the public.*

Ipswich Journal: April 8th 1780

*Saturday last, Jonathan Sawyer, alias Lock was executed at Rushmere near this town. He had hopes of life on the day he suffered, for when his irons were knocking off, he said he should not be hanged, that the Governor (meaning Mr. Ripshaw) had a reprieve in his pocket, but had a mind to see how he would behave. This notion persisted with him till his arms were pinioned and then he gave an account of more robberies he had committed, and of which he had before denied. It was observed by those that stood near him at the*

5

*place of execution that he did not once exchange countenance, and several times pulled up the hand kerchief that had been put over his face, and said he hoped his end would be a warning to others.*

Ipswich Journal: April 15th 1780

In all probability that was not the end of his grisly sentence, as the bodies of hanged felons could then be offered or even sold to doctors for dissection, sometimes conducted under the gaze of the public. The worst villains were gibbeted and their bodies hanged in chains for the crows to feed upon.

In November 1900, **Ellis Backler**, a 49 year old man from Haverhill was found guilty of a triple murder, that of his common-law wife and two of their children. He too received the full black-cap treatment, but he did not hang. By then, very few did. He was reprieved two weeks later on the grounds of his insanity, a defence that had saved a number, including the perpetrators of more celebrated killings, such as the Cretingham murder of 1887 and the Witnesham murder of 1896. Instead, he would be kept in secure accommodation for the rest of his life. At this time, though hanging in Suffolk would continue well into the twentieth century (3 hanged at Ipswich - in 1911, 1920 and 1924), it was common for submissions to be made to enable even the worst murderers to have their cases examined at the highest level. Execution, if it came to that, would be done as humanely as the technology allowed, and in private. By then, bodies of those executed would receive a proper inquest and a Christian burial.

At the end of this book is a spreadsheet of all cases coming before Suffolk Assize Judges in the period 1732 - 1900. Most of the information comes from local Suffolk newspapers of their day. For much of that time there are, at the very least, two surviving newspapers to refer to, regarding the trials. Such actual Assize records as survive in the Public Record Office at Kew are very incomplete and rarely give much information as to the outcomes of trials. By cross-referencing a number of newspapers, it has been possible to gather a much fuller picture, and though different papers may not agree on every detail, I am confident in the accuracy of practically everything listed here. Occasionally, other detail has been added from surviving trial lists, prison records, transportation lists and published trial accounts.

Capital offences on the statute book (those which carried the death penalty) increased throughout the eighteenth century until the early 1820s, by which time over 200 offences called for the full rigour of the law. These included *'going abroad with your face blackened'* (wearing a mask when conducting a robbery) and *'disguising oneself as an Egyptian'* (by which they meant a gipsy). In practice, few of those given death sentences in the early nineteenth century hung, as the very viable alternative of transportation to Australia was used more and more. This led the law into no small measure of disrepute. In the years 1820 & 1821, forty-two Suffolk criminals received death sentences, but only one was hanged (in his case, for burglary). It didn't make a lot of sense.

An Act of 1823 removed a large number of offences from the Capital List. These included *'stealing cloth from the rack or tenters in the night time',* and many varieties of theft from shops, warehouses, ships or docks. Also, it was no longer a hanging matter to kill deer, take rabbits from a warren or fish from a private river or pond. You could not be executed for rescuing people in custody for these offences, or for sending letters demanding money with threats of violence or false accusation. (For details, see the Bury Post: July 16th 1823)

Later 1820s courts introduced a two-tier system, distinguishing between the full *'Sentence of Death'* and the lesser *'Death Recorded.'* The truth of the matter is that little genuinely serious crime had troubled Suffolk for centuries. When **William Corder** was executed in August 1828 for the murder of Maria Marten in the Red Barn at Polstead, it was not just the horror of his crime that made it notorious, but the fact that he was the first murderer in Suffolk to hang for 13 years.

Rapidly, the number of capital offences declined, so by the early 1830s only about a dozen offences called for the death penalty, though rarely was execution enacted for anything other than murder after that point. *Arson* and *'An unnatural offence'* (sodomy) are exceptions to this rule, though no-one in Suffolk hanged for anything other than murder after 1835. The Criminal Law Consolidation Act of 1861 reduced these offences still further to Murder, Treason, Mutiny and Piracy.

Overall, the appended list at the back of this book contains nearly 1000 cases that definitely resulted in a death sentence of one kind or another. Of those, about 165 were hanged. Public hangings ended in 1868, **John Ducker** being the last in Suffolk, executed at Ipswich in April 1863 for the murder of a policeman in Halesworth. Of the names listed, just 55 are women, but a higher proportion of them hanged, fourteen in all. Their public hangings always drew a larger than average crowd. No woman was hanged in Suffolk after **Mary Cage**, who murdered her abusive husband in Stonham Aspal in 1851. Such was the tide of opinion at the time, she would almost certainly have had her sentence commuted, had her offence been as little as a year later. A select few feature on this list more than once, including the famous **Margaret Catchpole**, who received two death sentences before being transported to Australia.

## Capital punishment before 1770

Hangings accelerated during the eighteenth century and it is estimated the high point was between 1770 and 1830. In earlier times, it was felt that to enable justice to be seen to be done, punishment should be enacted as close as possible to the scene of the atrocity. Thieves were *'whipped at the cart's tail'* from the gaol to the place they had robbed and back again. Public exhibitions of justice were often on market day to attract the largest possible crowd. This system could mean occasional hangings in out-of-the-way places. **Tobias Gill**, described as a black drummer, responsible for rape and murder of a young girl at Blythburgh in 1750, was hanged there to appease local opinion, as this Ipswich Journal advertisement shows.

BLYTHBURGH, Sept. 5, 1750.
WHereas it was thought that TOBIAS GILL, the Black Drummer, who was condemn'd at Bury Assizes for the Murder of ANN BLAKMORE, would be executed at Ipswich; this is to inform the Publick, That he will certainly be executed at this Town, on Friday the 14th Instant, and afterwards will be hung in Chains near the Place where he committed the Fact.----He will be brought from Ipswich Goal to the Angel in this Town on Thursday the 13th Instant.

Such executions were rare in any one location, and drew a great deal of interest when they did occur. The Ipswich Journal published on April 10th 1742 brushed lightly over three hangings at Bury, giving more detail to an execution at Diss.

IPSWICH, *April* 9

We hear from BURY, that Reeve, Flower, and Townshend were executed there on Wednefday; and that the two firft feem'd to be very penitent, but Townshend fhew'd very little Senfe of his unhappy Condition.

*Extract of a Letter from* DISS, *dated April* 8.

' Laft Saturday Robert Carlton (who was condemn'd at
' the laft Thetford Affizes for Sodomy, and the Murder of
' a young Woman by Poifon) was brought hither from
' Norwich Caftle. Sunday in the Afternoon he was carried
' to Church, where an excellent Sermon, applicable to his
' Criminal's Condition, was preached before the largeft
' Congregation ever feen here. The next Day he was ex-
' ecuted upon our Common, and afterwards hanged in
' Chains. He behaved to the laft with very litfle fhew of
' Remorfe; and altho' he acknowledged the Sodomy, yet,
' when the Rope was about his Neck at the Gallows, he
' denied that he was guilty of the Murder. The People
' prefent at the Execution were computed by fome at
' 15,000, and by others at 20,000.'

Until 1752, a variety of felons could expect their bodies to be *'anatomised'* after death. From 1752 until 1834, the dissection of the body by doctors became a mandatory part of the sentence for murder, though often the gibbet was chosen instead. Gibbeting, or *'hanging the body in chains'* ended officially in 1832. Traitors (not a crime we encounter much in Suffolk at this time) were decapitated after hanging until 1820. Prisoners who tried to escape the hangman's noose by terminating their own existence (committing suicide) were often exhibited on a cart before being buried in a particularly barbaric way.

*Friday morning last, about six o'clock, when the turnkey of the New Gaol, Ipswich, went to Mann's cell, (who was to have suffered last Saturday for robbing Mr. Hart of Letheringham, on the highway) he found him hanging by a handkerchief against the wall. He immediately apprised the gaoler of it, who went to the cell, and cut him down, but all endeavours to restore him proved ineffectual. Same day, the Coroner's jury sat on the body and brought in their verdict Self-Murder; he was accordingly buried in the cross way with a stake driven through him.*

Bury Post: April 11th 1792

The burial of John Williams in 1811 after he cheated the hangman by committing suicide

In a strange case of 1779, **William Sell** and **John Carter** were found guilty of *'sodomitical practices.'* Thirty years later, it would have been a capital offence, but then resulted in a spell in the pillory. Even that proved too much for William Sell who took arsenic, but it had a delayed effect on him enabling him to serve his time in the pillory before he died. Then, we are told, as it was *'self murder'*, he was to be buried in the King's highway with a stake driven through his heart.

Though executions continued to rise throughout the eighteenth century, the percentage of those capitally convicted whose sentence was enacted diminished: in 1775, over half of all given death sentences nationwide actually hanged; by 1800, it was only a quarter; and continued to fall to about one in twenty by 1830.

Youth was not always a defence when charged with a capital offence. The following case is taken from The Newgate Calendar.

# WILLIAM YORK

*CONVICTED OF MURDER*

*This unhappy child was but just turned ten years of age when he committed the dreadful crime of which he was convicted. He was a pauper in the poorhouse belonging to the parish of Eye, in Suffolk,* [almost certainly, it was Eyke] *and was committed on the Coroner's inquest, to Ipswich gaol, for the*

*William York, aged Ten Years, murdering Susan Mahew, aged Five Years.*

*murder of Susan Mahew, another child, of five years of age, who had been his bed-fellow. The following is his confession, taken and attested by a justice of the peace, and which was, in part, proved on the trial, with many corroborating circumstances of his guilt.*

*He said that a trifling quarrel happening between them on the 13th of May 1748, about ten in the morning, he struck her with his open hand, and made her cry; that she going out of the house to the dunghill, opposite to the door, he followed her, with a hook in his hand, with an intent to kill her; but before he came up to her he set down the hook, and went into the house for a knife: he then came out again, took hold of the girl's left hand, and cut her wrist all round to the bone, and then threw her down, and cut her to the bone just above the elbow of the same arm... he cut her left thigh to the bone; and observing she was not dead yet, his next care was to conceal the murder; for which purpose he filled a pail with water at a ditch, and, washing the blood off the child's body, buried it in the dunghill, together with the blood that was spilled upon the ground, and made the dunghill as smooth as he could; afterwards he washed the knife and hook, and carried them into the house, cleaned the blood off his own clothes, hid the child's clothes in an old chamber, and then came down and got his breakfast. When he was examined, he showed very little concern, and appeared easy and cheerful. All he alleged was, that the child fouled the bed in which they lay together; that she was sulky, and that he did not like her.*

This *'boy murderer'* was found guilty, and sentence of death was pronounced against him; but he was respited from time to time, and, on account of his tender years, was at length pardoned, *"on condition of entering himself to serve His Majesty on board his fleet."* (Ipswich Journal: September 3rd 1757 - This report says he came from Eyke). The above account points out that Judge Hales ordered a boy of the same age to be hanged who burnt a child in a cradle. Also it recounts how two boys, small for their years, John Bunn (14) and Joseph Leech (15) were hanged at Tyburn for street robbery.

Reputedly, Michael Hammond, aged 7 and his 11 year-old sister were hanged at Lynn in 1708 for felony. If so, they were the youngest on record to hang. As late as 1831, a fourteen year-old lad called John Any Bell was executed in Kent for murder. As regards Suffolk, ages are not mentioned in a lot of the earlier cases, but death sentences were awarded to **George Mayes** (14) for housebreaking in Thornham Magna in 1808, **Joseph Bredfield** (14) for housebreaking in Eye in 1817, **John Webb** (14) for arson at Exning in 1819, **James Pleasants** (15) for arson at Lawshall in 1816, **George Jessup** (11) for stealing from a house in Rickinghall in 1826 and **Joseph Speller & George Jackson** (simply described as boys) for stealing silver in Bury in 1831.

The youth of a large number on the Suffolk list is a point worth noting. Two seventeen year-olds were hanged, **Maurice Griffin** for a murder commited in Woodbridge in 1814 and **William Aldous** for arson at Stradbroke in 1822, though these ages may not be correct. In addition, a number of other 'teenagers' were executed including two young women (**Sarah Lloyd** (19) and **Catherine Foster** (18)). Not until 1933, would a change in the law limit capital sentences to those over 18.

The closer you were to the person you abused, the worse the crime was believed to be. When **Charles Drew** shot and murdered his own father at Long Melford in 1740, his trial prompted the publication of broadsheets like the one below.

CHARLES DREW shooting his FATHER

THE 20
SUFFOLK PARRICIDE;
BEING, THE
TRIAL,
LIFE, TRANSACTIONS,
and LAST DYING WORDS,
OF
CHARLES DREW,

of *Long-Melford*, in the County of *Suffolk*;

Who was executed at *St. Edmund's-Bury*, on *Wednesday* the 9th of *April*, for the inhuman Murder of his Father, *Charles John Drew*, Esq; Attorney at Law, by shooting him thro' the Body, at his own House, on *Thursday* the 31st of *January* 1739-40.

CONTAINING.

1. An Account of his Extravagncies and Debaucheries which drove him to Necessity, and induced him to commit this horrid Fact.

2. The Scheme he laid to perpetrate it, his getting acquainted with John Humphreys; the Manner in which he prevailed upon him to undertake the Murder of his Father; and the Reasons that induced him thereto.

3. A particular Account of the Execution of the Fact, of Humphreys's refusing to do it, and of Charles Drew (the Son) taking the Musket from Humphreys, and shooting his Father.

ing a Reward for apprehending the Murderer, in order to screen himself, and take off the Suspicion of his being concerned.

5. The Means of discovering it by Mr. Mace, and true Copies of the Letters that were produced, and by which they got an Insight into the whole Affair.

6. The Manner in which it was discovered; an Account of Drew's Examination, and Copies of the Informations given before Col. de Veil, and his being sent to Newgate.

7. His Behaviour there, and endeavouring to corrupt Jonathan Keate, the Turnkey, to let him

If murder of a father was bad, a wife murdering her husband was far worse. In the eighteenth century, it counted as petty treason, and as such could mean a very different form of execution.

In April 1763, **Margery Bedingfield** was *'strangled and burnt to death'* on Rushmere Heath for the murder of her husband John Bedingfield of Sternfield in Suffolk. Her lover, **Richard Ringe** hanged for his part in the plot, but the law ordered that the faithless wife be burnt at the stake. In actual fact, it seems likely, she was tied to the stake by a rope around her neck and the stool she was standing on pulled away before the lighting of the faggots that were piled around her. The conspirators had been drawn up through the town on a *'sledge'* to enable them to experience the fullest humiliation possible.

In other parts of England, a similar fate could befall a servant that killed her master. In March 1731, the Ipswich Journal reported the execution of a servant named Mary Taylor, concerned in the murder of her mistress at Lynn in Norfolk. She was found guilty of petty treason, and sentenced to be burnt to ashes at a stake in Lynn. Her end was described in graphic detail in the papers of the time. Her male companion was hanged for the same offence.

A servant was supposed to be prepared to give her life to her mistress and this is probably why **Sarah Lloyd** was hanged for theft (and arson) in Hadleigh in 1800. The sentence reflected the horror felt at such a betrayal of trust.

Throughout history, extreme punishments have been seen as the only answer to certain kinds of crime, that now seem to us out of proportion to the crime committed. When **Arundel Coke** was tried for a violent attack on his brother-in-law, he offered an unusual defence. In 1721, Coke and his appointed *'hit-man,'* **John Woodburne** violently attacked Thomas Crispe in Bury St. Edmunds churchyard. They left him in a pool of blood, assuming he was dead. Horribly mutilated, he survived to give evidence against the two. Coke was a barrister and was horrified to discover he was being tried under the *'Coventry Act'* of 1671 of attempting to maim & disfigure Thomas Crispe. His plea was that rather than attempting to maim and disfigure him, he wanted to kill him, as attempted murder was not a capital offence at the time. There had been a number of high profile maimings, and the law had been strengthened to take account of the public horror of this.

John Woodburne had been promised twenty pounds and a house for his part in the affair. The two lost their case and they were both publicly hanged in Bury.

Crimes against property led to many a hanging. Burglary, stealing animals and highway robbery featured strongly in eighteenth century newspapers. As today, a small number of people could be responsible for a disproportionate amount of crime. In a desperate attempt to explain which of a notorious gang of robbers had been responsible for which crimes, the Norwich Mercury published this chart in 1751.

| 1. Mr. Ward, Nov. 26, 1748. | 2. Mrs. Leman, Dec. 5, 1748. | 3. Mr. Hall, Mar. 22, 1749. | 4. Mrs. Fentris, Oct. 9, 1750. | 5. Mr. Stubben, Oct. 19, 1750. | 6. Mr. Hempstead, Nov. 10, 1750. | 7. Mr. Fulcher, Dec. 22, 1750. |
|---|---|---|---|---|---|---|
| Mayhew, qu. | | Mayhew | Mayhew | Mayhew | Mayhew | Mayhew |
| Ja. Cunningham | Ja. Cunningham | Ja. Cunningham | Ja. Cunningham | Ja. Cunningham | | Ja. Cunningham |
| Jn. Cunningham | Jn. Cunningham | Jn. Cunningham | | Jn. Cunningham | Jn. Cunningham | Jn. Cunningham |
| Tho. Brook | Tho. Brook | Tho. Brook | | Tho. Brook | Tho. Brook | Tho. Brook |
| Catchpole, qu. | | | | Catchpole | Catchpole | Catchpole |
| Fisher, qu. | | Fisher | | Fisher | Fisher | Fisher |
| Button | Button | | | | | Button |
| Fidgett, qu. | | Fidgett | | | | Fidgett |
| | Cha. Blomfield | | | | | |
| | | James Brook | | | | |
| | | T. Cunningham | T. Cunningham | T. Cunningham | | T. Cunningham |

This was a bunch of criminals guilty of burglaries across East Anglia. In a number of cases, even those who confessed could not remember which offences they had carried out and with whom. Five met their end in Suffolk; others did so at Norwich and Tyburn.

Forgery and *'coyning'* (copying an image of the King's head in the forging of coins) were again regarded as treasonable acts and could lead to death by burning, though I have no evidence to show it did in this county. However, local papers in Suffolk and Norfolk reported the burning of Barbara Spenser at the stake in London in 1720 for such an offence.

Arson, especially after the invention of Lucifer matches, was a huge problem throughout the nineteenth century and saw a number of very young children indicted. The Assizes of 1844 were known as the *'Fiery Assizes'*, as most cases tried were for *'incendiarism.'*

Copy-cat crimes like this were an issue. 1836 saw a whole spate of sacrilege cases involving robbery from churches; fortunately for the participants, it was a crime that had been recently removed from the list of capital charges. The period 1828-36 saw a number of opportunist crimes - such as robbery whilst the family was in church, sometimes from the parson himself. Theft of livestock, especially horses led to the formation of protection groups along the lines of Farm-Watch, and led to many prosecutions, though only four hanged for animal theft out of a total of 43 executions carried out between 1780 and 1800. In 1832, animal theft ceased to be a hanging offence, followed by burglary and housebreaking in 1837, rape in 1841 and attempted murder in 1861. In reality, hangings for these offences had not been enacted for several years before their penalty was reduced. The same can be said of infanticide, a crime which spawned a number of high profile cases in the late nineteenth century, whereby (mostly single) mothers were accused of killing their new-born children. For all that, infanticide remained a capital crime until 1922.

The finality of a death sentence can make people reluctant to convict in cases where a lesser penalty might have obtained a conviction. Take, for example, the case of the Ipswich Press Gang murder. Towards the end of the eighteenth century, the country was desperate for sailors. Under a law of 1777, groups were empowered to *"impress such persons as could be found and enlist them on payment of one shilling into the service of the Admiralty."*

Realistically speaking, no-one in their right mind would take up the offer voluntarily, so press-gangs, eager to receive a bounty, would tour quayside taverns in the hope of abducting drunken men and pressing them into the service of the King.

On a night in January 1779, a gang of 17 entered the Green Man in Ipswich. They were recognised for what they were, and a riot broke out. Knives were drawn, even fire tools from the hearth were wielded by those anxious to escape the gang. In the subsequent affray, Thomas Nicholls was layed low by a blow to the head from which he did not recover. The seventeen men that made up the Press Gang were taken in for his murder. The Suffolk Record Office at Ipswich has a full account of the investigation and trial written by George Tebbing, the attending surgeon. One of the gang, **William Keeble**, died in gaol before he could be tried, but a true case was proved against the remaining sixteen. However, the

Judge was unwilling to sentence the men and passed the case to the King's Bench for review.

In the Ipswich Journal two months later, it was reported that as it was not possible to prove which of the men had caused Nicholls' death, or even if any of them had been responsible, they would all be freed. At the end of the day, they were not prepared to hang sixteen men for doing as the King ordered, even if their enthusiasm had got a bit out of hand. Their names were **Richard Hanton (a serving midshipman), John Bothwick, Edward Barry, Stephen Glanfield, Samuel Crouch, Stephen Richman, Benjamin Salmon, John Dale, Thos. Buxton, Thos. Marsh, Samuel Dunnet, Charles Cross, Jas. Firman, Robert Hanton, Joseph Grice & John Butcher.**

This was not a unique event as the Norfolk Chronicle on April 6th 1782 reported the death of George Clark, killed whilst being taken by the press-gang in a boat from Norwich to Yarmouth... *"the sail jibing it struck one of the men on the head, which knocked him overboard, and he was drowned."* He left a widow and four children in Drayton.

There was often a good deal of sympathy expressed for the condemned man or woman. The report of the trial and execution at Melton of **John Britt** of *'Capel near Butley'* in April 1736 dwelt on how his wife's nagging led him to murder her...

> *Upon some occasion, she provoked him very much with her tongue, for which he first turned her out of doors, but she came in again and gave him such ill language as he said he could not bear, but fell into a great passion in which he beat her immoderately, so that she died in two or three days of the bruises she received... He had the good word of his neighbours, who agreed he was highly provoked.*
>
> Suffolk Gazette: April 10th 1736

The description of the execution of **William Simpson** and **Joseph Lambert** of Hacheston for burglary in 1784 focuses on

the solemnity of the occasion, describing how the bells of each parish tolled as they passed from gaol in Ipswich to the gallows at Rushmere.

London executions describe a bell-man walking beside the cart used for transporting felons to their hanging.

Bell-man and cart are clearly visible in this illustration from the *'Newgate Calendar'*

Of course, not all Suffolk felons were tried in this county. A number spread their wings and put their dubious talents to use elsewhere. **Daniel Malden**, friend of Dick Turpin and later a London house thief, was an Ipswich man who came to prominence for escaping from Newgate Gaol twice, before suffering the inevitable penalty at Tyburn. Though forgotten in his own county of Suffolk, he still commands a whole page in *'The Oxford Dictionary of National Biography.'*

In 1750, three Suffolk men were hanged at Tyburn for smuggling and other offences. **Charles Gawen**, a shoemaker from Beccles, **John Carbold**, a baker from around Hopton-on-sea and **John Doe**, a sieve-maker from Stowmarket had become comrades in the smuggling trade in Great Yarmouth. For three years, they were hunted men until a party of dragoons caught them just outside Norwich and took them to Newgate, where they faced trial at the Old Bailey before hanging at Tyburn.

There exists in Ipswich Record Office, the transcript of a letter written by Rev. David Edwards, non-conformist minister of the Old Chapel, Tacket Street to Rev. Conder, Principal of Homerton College , Cambridge in 1766. It concerns the ministering to two condemned men in Ipswich. **John Francis** and **John Brook** were found guilty of housebreaking, *'stealing £100 from the house of Mr. D____.'* Reputedly, the owner had promised that if the money was returned, he would see the criminals did not hang, but of course it was out of his control, and the court had other ideas.

Rev. Edwards attended the men in prison and even arranged for them to be *'brought in chains through streets thronged with people'* to his chapel, where he preached a (hellfire?) sermon at them, causing them to *'shed an abundance of tears.'* He travelled with them to *'The Fatal Tree',* and spoke at length to the crowd, appealing to them to *'flee youthful lusts,'* and urging them to pray for the prisoners, his words being such that *'weeping spread itself over the face of the people.'* He wrote with some satisfaction, saying this had been a triumph for the word of God.

As formerly mentioned, everything was done to make the punishment visible and, as some believed, *'educational.'* Mothers took young children and there are many contemporary accounts of large crowds arriving early to ensure a good view. Newspapers were a bit slow on picking up on this, reporting thinly on most cases before 1800. By 1815, the majority of executions were given extensive coverage until the end of public hangings in 1868.

From about 1835, there was a strong drive to abolish hanging altogether and letters to the editor appeared regularly, especially at the times of executions. Leaflets were distributed amongst the crowds, and petitions raised. The following broadside, published by the London printer, Gilpin in 1847 to protest at the execution of **Catherine Foster** in Bury St. Edmunds, was typical.

---

### GRAND MORAL SPECTACLE!

Under the Authority of the Secretary of State for the Home Department

THIS DAY, SATURDAY, APRIL 17, 1847,

A YOUNG GIRL

SIXTEEN YEARS OF AGE

IS TO BE

PUBLICLY STRANGLED

IN FRONT OF THE

County Jail, Bury St Edmonds

SHE WILL APPEAR

Attended by a Minister of the Church of England,
clad in his Robes Canonical;

ALSO BY THE HANGMAN,

The Great Moral Teacher,

who after fastening her arms to her side, and putting a rope round her neck, will strike the scaffold from under her; and if the neck of the wretched victim be not by this shock broken, the said MORAL TEACHER will pull the legs of the miserable girl until by his weight and strength united he

STRANGLES HER

---

Broadsheets of a number of kinds had become popular as early as the sixteenth century. These would be sold at and after the hanging of notorious felons. Often illustrated, with songs or poems attached, they claimed to publish the last confession of the condemned man or woman, even if they refused to confess and professed their innocence to the last, as this verse of the song *'Clever Tom Clinch'* by Jonathan Swift (1723) shows…

*But, as from the windows the ladies he spied,*
*Like a beau in the box, he bow'd low on each side;*
*And when his last speech the loud hawkers did cry,*
*He swore from his cart, it was all a damn'd lie.*

In the case of multiple hangings, the pictured scene accompanying many such broadsheets carried an inserted engraving (such as is pictured below) that could contain either one, two, three or four nooses on the scaffold.

It was the job of the *'ordinary'* to obtain the condemned man's confession. Usually this was the prison chaplain, who could sell the confession to the printers. These men were not always highly respected as these passages from Moll Flanders (by Daniel Defoe, 1722) show.

> *The ordinary of Newgate came to me, and talked a little in his way, but all his divinity ran upon confessing my crime, as he called it (though he knew not what I was in for), making a full discovery, and the like, without which he told me God would never forgive me; and he said so little to the purpose, that I had no manner of consolation from him; and then to observe the poor creature preaching confession and repentance to me in the morning, and find him drunk with brandy and spirits by noon, this had something in it so shocking, that I began to nauseate the man more than his work, and his work too by degrees, for the sake of the man; so that I desired him to trouble me no more.*
>
> *...All the while the poor condemned creatures were preparing to their death, and the ordinary, as they call him, was busy with them, disposing them to submit to their sentence.*

From 1840, just about any hanging provoked a flurry of applications for mercy, with varied results. Sometimes it just meant a series of delays before a felon was finally *'turned off.'* **William Howell**, who shot a police constable at Gisleham in 1844, suffered a series of respites of sentence before hanging nearly six weeks later. Ironically, the Hessett highway robber **Simon Frost** who had been capitally convicted of one of a number of his crimes in Nowton in 1832 was reprieved following a petition raised by the inhabitants of Hessett where he lived. Their faith in him was ill judged as, on the way to New South Wales, under order of transportation, he killed a man and ended up being *'hanged from the yard-arm.'*

Escapes from gaol were quite common in the eighteenth century when both Ipswich and Bury gaols were far from secure. Four such stories are worth noting.

Ipswich Journal

**Thomas Bird** had been reprieved, following his death sentence for horse stealing and highway robbery at Ashbocking. The two escapees were under order of transportation, but this was after transportation to America had stopped and before Australian transports had begun. They committed a capital offence by escaping from a sentence of transportation. Fortunately for them, I can find no record of their being caught. They were never transported.

One intrepid convict who was recaptured was **Robert Caston** who had robbed the Ipswich Custom House in 1735. In December of that year, he escaped from Ipswich gaol whilst awaiting trial, stole a fishing boat and sailed to Calais, where word reached the authorities he might be there. When he tried to sell the boat, he was apprehended and returned to Ipswich for trial.

Escaping from the condemned cell did no harm to **William Maddox (alias Bolton)**. Tried and convicted for a burglary at Thwaite Buck's Head in 1773, he made his escape.

*Last Tuesday, about twelve at night, Wm. Bolton, a capital convict in the gaol in this town, and two other felons, having got off their irons, proceeded to the keeper's apartment, and with large knives and pistols, threatened him with immediate death if he gave the least alarm; they then took the keys and made their escape, and tho' diligent pursuit is making after them, they have not yet been so much as heard.*
- *See advertisement in the next page.* (in this case, below)

Ipswich Journal: April 10th 1773

WHEREAS the following Persons made their Escape out of Ipswich Goal, in the County of Suffolk, about Twelve o'Clock in the Night of the 6th of April instant;

WM. BOLTON, convicted at last Bury assizes of Housebreaking, is about 22 Years of Age, light-brown curled Hair, pock-pitted, about 5 Feet 8 Inches high, had on, when he went away, a blue Coat, black Waistcoat, Leather Breeches, and a small round Hat.

JOHN BROWNE, convicted at the last Sessions for the Borough of Ipswich, for a Robbery; is about 20 Years of Age 5 Feet 6 Inches high, full-faced, thick Lips, short dark-brown Hair, one Eye black from a Blow; had on when he went away a short red Soldier's Jacket, a white Linnen Waistcoat, and a Pair of old Leather Breeches; but it is supposed he now goes in a Butcher's Dress.

HENRY SMITH, committed for a Robbery at Debenham in this County; about 5 Feet 9 Inches high, very stout, round Shoulders, strait dark-brown Hair; had on, when he went away, a ribb'd Fustian Frock, a light Cloth Waistcoat, and Leather-Breeches.

Whoever will apprehend, and bring to the said Goal, the said Wm. Bolton, John Brown, and Henry Smith, shall receive for each of them so apprehended, the Sum of TWENTY GUINEAS Reward from me,

April 7, 1773.           JOHN BAKER, Goaler.

One of the escapers was recaptured later that year: Henry Smith went home to Debenham, was caught and sent back to prison (Ipswich Journal: July 10th 1773); but Bolton stayed at large for four years, and even went as far as America. Driven out by the War of Independence, he returned, only to be recaptured in London in 1777 (Ipswich Journal: March 8th 1777). He was again condemned to death, but this was twice respited, before he obtained a Royal pardon later that year, and walked away a free man. Perhaps he made the most of his new start. All this, in spite of the fact, in 1768, the Ipswich Journal had described him as being one of the most wanted criminals in the country. (June 18th)

The building of new gaols in Ipswich and Bury soon after 1800 cut escapes to a minimum, though strong walls would have done little to prevent this bid for freedom:

*Last week three prisoners here were condemned and ordered to be executed; but one of them dying the night before execution, and being put in a coffin, one of the others found means to convey his body and laid himself in its place, so that at midnight, when the jailers thought to carry out the body in order for interment, the fellow no sooner found himself    without the walls of the prison, than he began to make a noise and so frighted the bearers that they threw the coffin off their shoulders and ran away, which gave him the opportunity     he wanted to open the lid and make his escape.*

Suffolk Gazette: August 9th 1736

Crime drew crowds at every stage. The Assizes, initially at Bury, later shared between Bury and Ipswich, attracted huge numbers to the town where the trials were being heard. Hangings drew still greater numbers. There are reports of special trains being run to transport thousands to the public executions of **Mary Cage** (Ipswich 1851) and **James Bloomfield Rush** (Norwich 1849). With such interest came classic scenes of nineteenth century melodrama, with prisoners pleading for their lives on bended knees, and curses being uttered at those testifying against them.

The courtroom melodrama was never more in evidence than at the trial of **William Gibbs**, a soldier convicted of highway robbery at Kesgrave in 1802, when we are told… *"His Lordship burst into tears and all joined in."* It was felt that this was a case where a fundamentally good man had behaved in a manner totally out of character, putting his very life at risk. Gibbs was reprieved and given a prison sentence instead.

During the period of the Napoleonic Wars, Suffolk was full of army camps. Serving men had often been paid a bounty to join up. Much of the crime at that time involved soldiers or ex-soldiers. **William Holmes**, described as a pauper in the House of Industry at Melton was convicted of feloniously assaulting a child under ten years of age, Elizabeth Eade, with intent to commit a rape. Four other similar indictments were preferred against him involving other children. At his execution in August 1805…*"a vast concourse of spectators attended."* It was said…

> *"His behaviour since his condemnation and at the place of execution was truly penitent and exemplary. He was former-ly a soldier in a regiment of foot and had lost a leg and thigh in the service of his country."*
>
> (Ipswich Journal: August 31st 1805)

Some of the worst criminals were not so much professional soldiers as serial joiners of regiments.

> *Saturday, **Thomas Hedgson, Isaac Blomfield and William Gowen** were executed at Rushmere near this town. On the evening before… Hedgson then delivered an ample confession of his numerous transgressions during the course of eight years… and desired it might be published; by which it appears that he had enlisted 49 times, from the different regiments in England, Scotland and Ireland, and had obtained thereby 397 guineas, bounty money. He seldom stayed more than a day before he deserted, and often enlisted two or theee times into another party of the same regiment on recruiting service at a*

*distance...* (This account then goes on to list his other crimes committed whilst on the run as a repeated deserter.)

Ipswich Journal: April 28th 1787

As mentioned earlier, grisly things were often done to hanged felons' bodies after their deaths. Thieves could be treated with more respect than murderers, though this was not necessarily true on every occasion. Early reports do not always give us as much detail as they did in the following case.

### Ipswich

*Last Saturday was Executed here* **George Chandler** *for horse stealing. All the time he lay under condemnation, he behaved in a very audacious manner... he was resolved to die intrepid. At the Place of Execution, he took no Notice of his Salvation, but requested of several Persons to see him buried at the Town from whence he came, which was denied him, on which he was buried near the gallows.* (He came from Saxtead, near Framlingham)

Suffolk Gazette: April 17th 1736

Other offenders were less fortunate. When **Ann Arnold** was convicted of murdering her bastard child by throwing him into a pond at Spexhall in 1812, there were many who sympathised with her as she had been abandoned by the child's father and was at her wits' end. It didn't prevent the full force of the law being invoked and...

*In the afternoon, her body was dissected in the Shire Hall, and we are sorry to observe crowds of women and children going thither to view so disgusting a sight. In the evening, her remains were interred in St. Margaret's churchyard.*

Ipswich Journal: April 3rd 1813

A contemporary illustration
of such a dissection

Even that seems mild compared to the treatment meeted out in some of the worst cases. Take for example the execution of **John Rye** for murder in 1777 in Norwich, where a most graphic account found its way into the local paper.

*The populace expressed the most indignant resentment against this horrid murderer by pulling and tossing the body whilst hanging, and after it was cut down, the carcass was with difficulty conveyed back to the prison, where it was kept till evening, and then carried to the Norfolk & Norwich Hospital. And on Thursday, after the head was scalped and the skull sawn through, a lecture was given by Mr. Donne upon the brain, with its meninges, and the nerves detached therefrom; yesterday, the lungs and the heart of this barbarous miscreant were taken out and dissected, and the great blood vessels issuing from thence, exposed to view. This day, the other cavity of the body will be cut open, and the liver, with other abdominal viscera, dissever'd from their attachments, in conformity to the sentence, which was wisely enacted by the legislature in 1752.*

Norfolk Chronicle: March 22nd 1777

*Cambridge*

*After the execution of Weems on the 6th inst. for the murder of his wife, the body was removed to the Chemical Lecture Room in the Botanical Garden, where Professor Cumming had prepared his powerful galvanic battery and made several experiments in that curious process which occasioned various movements resembling animation. The body was afterwards dissected by Mr. Okes.*

Bury & Norwich Post: August 18th 1819

This Frankenstein-like teatment was not restricted to surrounding counties. The body of **William Corder** was wired up in a similar way after his execution for the murder of Maria Marten at Polstead in 1828.

Even those were mild by comparison with this account of an Irish execution, reported in the Suffolk Mercury in 1731.

*DUBLIN*

*This day, **James Monaghan**, the butcher was hang'd and quartered at Stephen's Green for the murder of his wife: The Hangman rode to the execution in a suit of flowered fustian, presented to him by the Master Weavers... The Hangman, after the execution, made a tour with his bloody cleaver to the wonderful satisfaction of the inhabitants, who followed him in vast crowds with loud Huzzas.*

Suffolk Mercury: June 28th 1731

Occasionally, deals were struck with condemned prisoners. Norfolk and Suffolk papers in March 1731 reported one **Charles Ray** in Newgate under sentence of death arranging a free pardon for agreeing to a surgeon operating on his eardrum to find a cure and cause of deafness. This arrangement proved too much even for the sensibilities of those days and Ray was given his pardon without having to undergo the horrors of the surgeon's knife.

Executions were events that gave an opportunity for the poor and the disabled to make a few pence. Traditionally, blind beggars were the ballad singers of their day. Though broadsides would be

Blind Beggar ballad singers of the late eighteenth century

written for each hanging, there were songs that were sung at every such event, and crowds fuelled by drink would carouse around the town led in song by blind singers playing primitive instruments

# 𝕿𝖍𝖊 𝕳𝖆𝖓𝖌𝖒𝖊𝖓

More often than not, the hangman's real name was not mentioned when executions were reported in the eighteenth and early
nineteenth centuries. Generally, they seem to have been known
by the generic title, *'Jack Ketch,'* after an earlier executioner,
notorious for his barbaric inefficiency. The one on this occasion
does not seem to have been a lot better.

*Saturday last,* **Tho. Clarke, Tho. Carty and John Deane** *were
executed at Rushmere, near this town, for shooting at and
robbing Tho. Marsh, mariner at Yoxford. These men at the
place of execution behaved with astonishing resolution. After
having been assisted at prayers, and two psalms had been
sung, Jack Ketch was expected to put a final end to the
melancholy business, but he having forgot the halters, was
gone to Ipswich for them. This very extraordinary and unac-
countable forgetfulness caused a delay of near 20 minutes.
In this dreadful suspense, the unhappy objects exhibited no
particular marks of uneasiness. When the executioner got
upon the cart, they all stood up; and everything being now
ready for the awful moment, they joined hands, repeated the
Lord's Prayer, and then said they wished they might never
enter the kingdom of Heaven if they robbed Marsh! Clarke
died very hard, owing to the rope having been improperly
fixed from the trepidity of the hangman, who might be said to
shake like an aspen leaf; Deane, when he felt the cart move,
threw himself backward, but this did not accelerate his death,
as he appeared to be as much convulsed as the former; Carty
was not seen to move. These 3 men, whose ages together did
not amount to 63, were interred in one grave in St. Matthew's
churchyard the next morning.*

*Substance of the trial of the above persons, and the
particulars of their very extraordinary behaviour, on the*

*evening previous to their execution, may be had of the news-*
*men, price one penny.*

Ipswich Journal: August 6th 1785

(A copy of this trial document can be viewed at Ipswich Record Office)

The job of the executioner covered more than the occasional hanging. Prisoners were routinely flogged and branded.

Also, those who refused to plead had to be dealt with…

*Justice Barker's Maid of Chiswick, was try'd for the Murder of her Bastard Child, and was acquitted;* **And one Mary Andrews, being indicted of Felony refused to plead, but after the Executioner had thrice drawn her Thumbs with Whipcord, she submitted to plead, and was acquitted for Want of Evidence.**

Ipswich Journal: May 27th 1721

*At the trial, at the Guildhall, London,* **John Vernon alias Long Jack** *refused to plead in a case of housebreaking. As the law was then, his refusal meant that he should undergo the torture of being pressed to death.* (heavy stones being put on his chest) *So he was remanded back to Newgate and the press ordered to be fixed in order for his being press'd on Thursday morning; when being carried to the bar to receive sentence, the dread of the press had such influence on him that he thought fit to stand his trial.*

Suffolk Gazette: August 31st 1736

…as a result of which he was found guilty and hanged at Tyburn.

As time progressed, certain executioners became celebrities of a kind and their names were known around the counties they served. One such was **William Calcraft** (in office 1829 - 1874). Coming from Little Baddow in Essex, he was official hangman at Newgate Gaol in London. His retainer and wages there would not have been very high, but he could charge at least ten guineas a hanging elsewhere. As a result, he travelled the south of England, plying his trade for forty-five years. He favoured a short drop, which meant his victims strangled to death slowly. There were perks to the position. In some places, he was allowed to keep clothes and personal effects belonging to the prisoners. These, along with pieces of the hang-rope were in great demand as souvenirs, especially in the most famous cases.

Calcraft was succeeded by **William Marwood**, (in office 1874 - 1883) whose procedure was more humane, as he favoured using a long drop. By this time, of course, all executions were in private, within the prison walls, though the press and witnesses were often invited. Subsequent executioners were less well known. They became shadowy figures, whose names were rarely reported.

Felons were not always hanged singly. In the late eighteenth and early nineteenth centuries, multiple hangings were not uncommon. At Newgate, as many as 20 were hanged in one day. Not since the days of the Witch-finder General were numbers like that hanged in Suffolk. However, in 1785, seven hanged in Ipswich and one in Bury. In April 1824, four hardened criminals were hanged on the same day at Bury St. Edmunds.

Around 1814, in the course of about 12 months three women were hanged for the murders of their bastard children, giving Ipswich the unpleasant reputation as the national centre for infanticide. Before convicting four miscreants who were to hang at Ipswich in 1812 (three for murder and one for rape & incest), Justice Heath observed... *"in the whole circuit he had not seen such a calendar of so black and such heinous crimes - It was melancholy proof of the depravity of the lower orders of this county."*

(Ipswich Journal: March 28th 1812)

It is true, most of those convicted were from the very bottom of the social scale. The newspapers seem to have taken a delight in describing the depths to which such people could sink...

*Saturday last, **John Took** was executed here, pursuant to his sentence (for the rape of his daughter at Melton). His behaviour to the last exhibited strong indications of extreme ignorance and insensibility. His wife and four children were in the crowd collecting money; but before he was turned off, the Sheriff ordered two constables to take them out of sight of the place of execution.*

Ipswich Journal: April 18th 1812

Hangings were quite rare in Suffolk after 1851. Only ten men were executed at Ipswich after that point. The last to be executed at Bury was **George Carnt** in 1851, and the last woman to hang in Suffolk was **Mary Cage** at Ipswich that same year.

There were a number of beliefs attached to the whole process of execution, and in particular, the hanged man himself. Some of these are reminiscent of the days of witchcraft trials. There were those who believed that a murderer could cause the corpse of his victim to bleed and he could be put to the test in this way. There are cases where the accused asked to touch the murder victim in the belief it would demonstrate his innocence.

It was widely believed that the body of the victim possessed healing powers, and to touch him soon after his hanging could be of benefit in the cure of any number of ailments. Here was another opportunity for the hangman to make a little extra from the event. Being at the front of the crowd at an execution wasn't only to allow you to get a good view.

'A touch of healing' a cartoon by Thomas Rowlandson.

Though this next story is not set in Suffolk, it is from one of our local papers and gives another indication of the superstitions surrounding hanging.

*DUBLIN - Wednesday, **John Duff**, convicted of robbing the mail on Kilmainham road, and whose execution had been respited from Saturday last, was brought to the gallows at Stephen's Green, where he declared in a most solemn manner his innocence of the crime for which he was condemned to suffer; after some time spent in praying, he was turned off, and having hung the usual time, was cut down, and being put in a coffin was carried away by his friends. It has been a practice lately, though hitherto without effect, for the populace to endeavour, by bleeding, chasing &c. to recover those unhappy objects to life; in this case, however, their experiments were successful, for after bleeding him, a pulsation was observed, upon which he was conveyed to the fields of Portabello, where in less than two hours, he exhibited several convulsive motions, opened his eyes, and breathed freely. Further assistance being given him, he was restored to an existence, the final period of which, it is hoped, will not be marked with the ignominy he suffered.*

Ipswich Journal: August 2nd 1777

Unfortunately...

*John Duff, [the same John Duff] who was hanged at Stephen's Green (Dublin) for robbing the mail, after being cut down was let blood in a field, and brought alive to a cabin near Milltown, where being too plentifully supplied with whiskey, the bandage came off his arm in the night, and a violent haemorrhage ensued, of which he died about 3 o'clock on Thursday, solemnly declaring his innocence.*

Ipswich Journal: August 9th 1777

# The Suffolk County Assizes

Shire Hall Bury St. Edmunds

The reporting of Assize trials improved as the nineteenth century unfolded. New papers came into being, so that soon after the end of public hangings in 1868, there were over 20 titles being published weekly in Suffolk, as well as a couple of dailies. As education improved, more people wanted to read them, and what most of them specialised in was the reporting of crime.

Serious crime was handled in the Assize Courts before a High Court Judge and a carefully selected jury. Most of the years covered in this book saw two Assize gatherings a year. Originally, these were held at the Old Shire Hall, Bury St. Edmunds, but as the 1800s progressed, Ipswich shared the Assizes with Bury. From 1839 until 1869, Summer Assizes were at Ipswich, Spring Assizes at Bury; after 1869, this was reversed.

Two Assizes were held, usually in March and July except on rare occasions when an extra Assize was deemed necessary, as in 1844, as a spate of high profile cases required attention. Towards the end of the nineteenth century, Assizes were increased to four a year, so prisoners would not have to wait so long on remand. However, a few empty sessions led them to try combining Norfolk and Suffolk courts. Even this proved less than efficient when

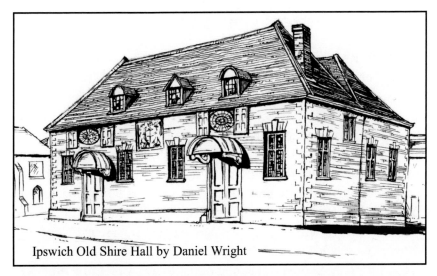
Ipswich Old Shire Hall by Daniel Wright

disproportionate numbers of Norfolk felons were being brought to Suffolk for trial, whilst Suffolk gaols remained fairly devoid of serious cases.

As we neared the end of the century, the compromise had been reached whereby it was agreed, Norfolk & Suffolk should have separate courts three times a year. By this time, very few cases were incurring the severest penalty.

## Elizabeth Burroughs & Henry Steward
## ~ tried for the murder of Mary Booty in March 1766

This was an odd case with an unsatisfactory conclusion that refused to be forgotten. Henry Steward was an upholsterer in Bury. He employed a few servants, one of whom was to become the victim. Elizabeth Burroughs appears to have broken into the house, climbing in through the window, but was spotted and escaped, having first tangled with Mary. It was left to the jury to decide whether Mary's fatal injuries had been inflicted by Elizabeth Burroughs or, as she suggested, by Henry Steward. Motives were hard to find, but as this case was investigated, tried and dealt with in less than a month, there was little time for thoroughness. Steward was declared 'not guilty', and Elizabeth Burroughs went to the gallows still protesting her innocence. When asked to confess, she replied, *"Would you have me die with a lie in my mouth? I die innocent of the crime as the child unborn."*

The following year, a woolcomber by the name of Samuel Otley was questioned in Bury, having confessed to being Mary Booty's killer. He was dismissed as insane and *'orders were given for his being properly taken care of.'*

Still much was left unexplained, but it is interesting to note that the pamphlet at Bury Record Office chronicling the events of this crime was published forty years later, just after the death of Henry Steward. It hinted again at his part in Mary Booty's death. On the assumption that you can't libel the dead, the publisher had timed the reopening of the mystery to perfection.

## Lay & Hoy ~ Hanged April 10th 1779

William Lay and Robert Hoy were separately convicted of burglary: Lay had broken into countless houses in Ipswich; Hoy was less of a hardened criminal but had broken into a house in Brantham. They received the full black-cap treatment, but the Ordinary at Ipswich gaol, Rev. Richard Brome, obtained a respite of seven days for Hoy. The Sheriff, out of consideration, deferred the hanging of William Lay. It was only a temporary respite, and they knew it. With a little help from their friends, the two broke out of the gaol and made off across Ipswich, with Mr. Ripshaw the prison governor in hot pursuit. He was probably fitter than two men who had been living on a prison diet for a while. The two cut across the garden of the Black Horse, threatening the landlord and pushing his face into the mud. Hoy, however, took a tumble and was caught. Lay was found hiding in a privvy in St. Matthews Street. Back at prison, they were double-ironed. They had escaped through a hole they had cut through the wall of their cell, covering it with a towel to avoid its discovery. A friend by the name of James Spooner was tried at the next Assize for aiding in their escape, but was acquitted. Lay played the tough-guy up to the last, when all the courage drained out of him. As the rope was put around his neck, he was reported as saying, *"Lord Jesus Christ! Where am I going?"*

## May & Theobald ~ Hanged March 23rd 1783

In October 1782, James May (alias Folkes) and Jeremiah Theobald (alias Hasel) murdered a sheep farmer by the name of Mrs. Phillips at Eriswell near Mildenhall. According to their testimony, they had been led to believe by Richard Munson (or Munsell) that she had a great deal of money in her house, and were determined to have it. Munson thought better of getting involved with these two, and later it was his evidence that helped to convict them.

> *When Theobald, now in custody for the murder of Mrs Phillips at Eriswell, was in the cart and being brought to Bury Gaol, he addressed himself to Munsell who had been concerned with May and Theobald in other offences but who had refused to take part in the last iniquitous act and turned evidence against them, saying, "damn you Munsell, I am sure of death, but you shall not live for long."*

Bury Post: November 14th 1782

Another colleague turned informer was Benjamin Wiseman, who got just two years for receiving the proceeds of an earlier robbery.

Mrs. Phillips had been roused in the night by cries claiming a dog was among her sheep. She lived at a house known as *The Croft* and farmed two pieces of land called *The Dolvers* in the village of Eriswell. According to the court reports, Wiseman was given the job of keeping her quiet whilst the other two robbed the house. Her death was from a mixture of strangulation and a blow from a blunt object. Later, Wiseman would confess it was he who had strangled her, causing her death. But by then it was too late for his colleagues. Theobald was well known to the court. Previously sentenced to death for a burglary in Long Melford, he had been allowed, as an alternative, to enlist as a soldier. The defence tried to discredit the two witnesses, whom they said were lying to save their own necks, but this worked against May and Theobald as the judge said the badness of their character was evident from the company they chose to keep. On the jury finding them guilty in less than half an hour, the judge passed sentence, saying, '*they had been moved and seduced by the instigation of the Devil* and        recommended them to *make the most of the short time they had to live, that they might obtain that mercy in another world which   justice demanded them not to expect in this.*' (Bury Post: March 26th 1783)

May's confession, delivered the night before his execution, was reported in the Bury Post of March 26th 1783. It implicated Richard Munson and Benjamin Wiseman strongly in the crime.

May & Theobald were hanged less than 48 hours after they had received sentence, and their bodies given to the surgeons to be anatomised, after which "*at the particular request of the prosecutor, they were afterwards hung in chains near the spot where the murder was committed.*"

### James Steggles ~ Hanged April 2nd 1783

At the same Assize, *"James Steggles was indicted for wilfully and maliciously shooting at WILLIAM MACRO with a pistol loaded with gunpowder and a leaden slug on the King's highway in the parish of BARROW in the county of SUFFOLK on the 6th day of January 1783."*

Mr. Macro, *"a considerable farmer"*, was returning on foot from a tything meeting at the Red Lion at Barrow, when he was attacked by a thief with a gun. By all accounts, he was remarkably lucky. Though the gun was fired at point-blank range, the charge missed him, but was close enough to leave a piece of wadding in his wig. *"D___n you! Your money or your life!,"* the thief had demanded.

Steggles made off in the direction of Kentford, but the horse he had borrowed was tired and he got no further than the Kentford Bull, where he was finally arrested. Three others in that court were found guilty of the crime of Highway robbery, but this shooting shocked the officials of the court and Steggles hanged for his recklessness.

### John & Elizabeth Wilkinson ~ Hanged March 28th 1785

In a case that was one of appalling neglect rather than deliberate murderous intent, the Wilkinsons were tried for the murder of their daughter, Martha. The couple from the then tiny fishing village of Felixstowe had cruelly treated this child from John Wilkinson's previous marriage. They appear to have made little attempt to defend themselves against the charges and went meekly and penitently to their deaths.

*Monday last, John Wilkinson and Elizabeth his wife were executed at Rushmere, near this town for the murder of*

*Martha, their youngest daughter. The bell tolled them out of town, and Wilkinson's wife read as she went along. When she came within sight of the gallows, she pulled off her cloak and gave it to her sister. At the place of execution, the Rev. Mr. Brome prayed with them; which being ended, the woman shook hands with every person within her reach. She then called Mr. Ripshaw* [prison governor] *to her, and asked him if she ever behaved indecently whilst in his custody. Who told her no. After this, she was for sitting down to pray longer, but her husband told her it was time to stand up. They then addressed the numerous spectators, declaring their innocence ...The hangman, in fixing the halter about their necks, trembled very much; this not escaping their notice, they desired him to do his duty, saying, they owed him no ill-will. In fact, there was not the least sign of fear or trembling in them, through the whole of this trying scene; and had they been persons of education, their behaviour would have favoured more of firmness than obstinacy in their last moments. They died without pity (particularly the woman) it being the general opinion, that a more cruel wretch has not existed since the days of Mrs Brownrigg. After hanging the usual time, Wilkinson's body was delivered to Mr. Bucke of this town, and his wife's to Mr. Abbot of Needham, for dissection.*

Ipswich Journal: April 2nd 1785

## John & Elizabeth Smith ~ Hanged March 23rd 1812

This story bears such similarity to the previous one, it makes sense to insert it here. Mary Ann Smith, at the age of 8 had died after being subjected to a regime of beating, starving and exposure to cold. John Smith, her father had remarried following the death of his first wife. He already had three children. This second marriage brought about terrible changes to the lives of those children, especially, Mary Ann, the eldest. She was said to have become emaciated, and her feet were so frost-bitten, she died from infections that set in. This case shocked the county. Though the step-mother was largely responsible for the child's state, nobody could forgive the father for failing to notice what had been happening to his child. At the end, he appeared to take the burden of guilt as both were sentenced to death...

*"Smith and his wife have not spoke together for some time, and during the trial, they never even glanced at each other. The man seemed much affected during the trial, and particularly so whilst the judge was passing sentence, when he wept bitterly. The woman prisoner, on the contrary, seemed indifferent to either the trial or the sentence, and never moved a muscle."*

This extract is taken from a booklet published at the time, priced one shilling, printed by Mr. Gedge, proprietor of the Bury Post. It can be viewed at Bury Record Office.

The two Smiths hanged at Ipswich on the same day as Edmund Thrower, whose crime is also described in this book.

## William Mayhew ~ Sentenced to death March 1789

Arrested and tried for robbery at Brent Eleigh in 1789, William Mayhew was set to hang at Bury St. Edmunds on April 15th. This date had been set far enough away from the trial to enable a reprieve to be sought. On April 8th, the Bury Post reported that a respite of one month had been allowed, to petition His Majesty George III over the matter. Two months later, the following report appeared.

*His Majesty has been pleased to grant a pardon to William Mayhew, under sentence of death for robbing the house of Col. Goate, on condition of his being transported to the coast of Africa for life.*

Bury Post: June 17th 1789

Transportation was having a few problems at the time. Following the American War of Independence, we could no longer

48

send convicts to Virginia. Though the West coast of Africa was considered, the heat and the disease meant it was not to be a serious option.

The First Fleet had just sailed with convicts to Botany Bay in Australia, and though it would be some years before this gained momentum, prison hulks were rapidly filling up with criminals awaiting transportation. Ports such as Portsmouth and Chatham had large numbers of such ships anchored just offshore. Many of the convicts served out their sentences of transportation there, working in the docks.

William Mayhew, however, was finally transported to New South Wales in January 1791.

### John Dowsing ~ Hanged August 5th 1789

It was said at his trial that John Dowsing had been responsible for the death of Ann, his second wife, *"by choaking and strangling her."* What comes through in this trial is just how close people must have been living to one another in the slums of Halesworth in the eighteenth century. Every sound of the Dowsings' arguments had been heard by a host of neighbours who lived little more than a wall's thickness away. Everyone said that although they had lived together for ten or eleven years, *"they had lived together on very bad terms."*

At his execution, Dowsing continued to claim his innocence, but acknowledged *"he justly merited such a death for the transgressions of his life."* (Trial report: Ipswich Record Office)

### John & Nathan Nichols ~ Hanged March 29th 1794

This was an odd case, as there appeared no reason for a fifty-nine year old man from Fakenham Magna and his nineteen year old son to murder John Nichols' daughter Sarah. They appear to have met the girl as she returned with a *'poke of flour'* that she had been sent for. Then, according to testimony, Nathan on his father's instruction took a stick from the hedgerow and beat the child to death with it. They then tied a garter around her neck and threw her into a ditch *"to make it appear she had strangled herself."*

The son changed his story several times during questioning and though he appeared to implicate his father, later he claimed it had been his work entirely. The father's reaction to learning of his daughter's death did not help his case. He seemed a long way from the grief-stricken parent that was expected.

The two were damned by the judge's summing up, where he virtually told the jury the two had demonstrated *"spleen, malice, rancour and hatred,"* and regardless of the son's changing confession, it was aided by *"a chain of striking and corroborating circumstances."*

*"The murder you have committed"*, His Lordship told the two on sentencing them, *"is of a most aggravated and extraordinary nature; that a father should aid and abet his own son in murdering a daughter is an instance of such depravity I have never before witnessed in the office I now hold."*

He then suggested they prepare themselves for divine judgement as their life on Earth was nearly at an end. There was a distinction between those receiving capital sentences. Murderers like John and Nathan Nichols were to be hanged within 48 hours, as there was no hope of a reprieve. Those to be hanged for lesser offences could find a delay of several weeks. John Nichols continued to claim his innocence to the last. His son Nathan, possibly in an attempt to save his father, told spectators at his execution that his father was innocent, and he alone did the crime. The two gave their hats to the hangman before being *"launched into eternity."*

John Nichols' body was carried to Honnington to be hung in chains, while the son's body was taken to the Shire Hall *"to be publicly dissected and anatomised."*

## Charles Blyth & James Dosser ~ Hanged August 15th 1795

The execution of these two saw a change in the way such matters would be conducted in Ipswich. Gone was the cart taking them up to Rushmere. Gone was the tolling of bells from parish to parish. A drop was built in front of the gaol and the scene enacted there before *"a vast number of spectators."* Blyth, at 40, was a regular in Suffolk courts, having stolen no less than fourteen horses in the course of his life. Dosser, a married man with two children was a master staymaker from Woodbridge who had turned to burglary.

> *They were attended by the Ordinary. After about 20 minutes spent in prayer, they mounted the drop with hasty steps, and with their faces towards the gaol, were turned off without uttering a word. Blyth was dead in an instant; but his companion was 7 minutes and a half in dying. These unhappy men were the first ever executed on a drop in this place.*
> Ipswich Journal: August 22nd 1795

## Margaret Catchpole
## ~ Sentenced to death: August 1797 and August 1800

The following story first appeared in local papers in May 1797. *Yesterday se'nnight, a coach-horse belonging to John Cobbold Esq. of Ipswich, was stolen out of his stable by a woman who formerly lived servant with him, and who rode the horse from Ipswich to London, it is supposed, in about ten hours, where she offered him for sale to a stable keeper, who gave notice thereof at one of the Public offices. In consequence she was apprehended, and, it is expected, will be shortly removed by a Habeas to Ipswich, in order to take her trial at the next Assizes. She was dressed in man's apparel when she rode off with the horse.*

Bury Post: May 31st 1797

So began a tale that was to be told over and over again. Though her name was omitted from this early account, Margaret Catchpole would soon become famous. Later, she would become the subject of a best-seller by the Reverend Richard Cobbold, though his book made much of the romance of the tale, often at the expense of the truth. Though some accounts add credence to Cobbold's story by saying he was her former employer, he was in fact a new-born child when she first came to trial.

A number of attempts have been made to unravel fact from fancy regarding Margaret Catchpole, and it is probably fair to say that without Cobbold's book, she would probably have been long forgotten as are so many in the list at the end of this book. It was the tale of triumph over adversity that has struck a chord with readers from Victorian times until the present day.

In truth, Margaret was born at Hoo in Suffolk in 1762, spending her formative years living with her uncle, William Leader at Brandeston. Much is made of Margaret's relationship with a smuggler by the name of Will Laud. Smuggling did not just involve ships and the bringing ashore of goods. There needed to be a whole network of contacts and distributors across the county. At the time when Margaret lived in Brandeston, one of the most notorious smugglers of his day lived there, a man called George Cullum. Many accounts assume Margaret was not involved with her smuggler until she moved into service at Nacton. It is far more likely she was already well acquainted with the smuggling community, as *'Cullum's banditi'* were a focus for the distribution of smuggled goods across the county.

BRANDESTON.
Where Margaret Catchpole lived with her Uncle Leider.

Later, employed in Ipswich by the Cobbold family, Margaret was responsible for the horse-stealing incident reported on the previous page. It appears that Elizabeth Cobbold spoke up for her, and her first death sentence was commuted to 7 years' transportation.  At that time, it took a while for convicts to find themselves on their way to Botany Bay (it could be a delay of up to 5 years).

In 1800, as the reward notice below shows, Margaret escaped, prompting, on her recapture, another death sentence, which was again commuted to one of transportation.

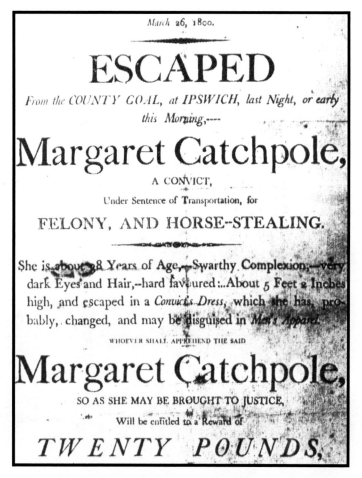

It is interesting to read her description.  Cobbold's book describes her as being tall, young, pretty and well educated.  In actual fact, she was barely literate, 'hard favoured', and looking older than her 38 years.

Margaret escaping from Ipswich gaol

Newspaper accounts describe her being taken near Shingle Street by Mr. Ripshaw of Sudbourn. His name has already featured in this book. He was, of course, governor of Ipswich Gaol. Her lover, Will Laud, by all accounts, was killed. They had been attempting to escape by boat to the continent. The next boat she would board would be the Nile, a prison hulk bound for Australia. She never returned, but died there in 1819.

### Sarah Lloyd ~ Hanged April 23rd 1800

Even for such early times, this was a case that left a bad taste in the mouth, so to speak. Sarah Lloyd, just 19, was arrested in October 1799. The charges against her included arson, burglary and attempted murder. It was said at her trial, she, together with her lover, Joseph Clark, stole from her employer, Mrs. Syer of Hadleigh in Suffolk, and to cover their tracks set fire to the building. Fortunately, neighbours alerted Mrs. Syer to the fire and helped her to escape. At the Assize in April 1800, the charges of arson and attempted murder were never brought. Sarah was found to be innocent of burglary, but guilty of larceny to the value of 40 shillings. No case could be proven against her lover, though it was generally believed he had been the driving force behind the crime. As has been shown, it was common for people to receive death sentences for fairly trivial crimes, only to find their sentence reduced to one of imprisonment or transportation. Whilst nobody was denying her guilt, most must have expected Sarah's death penalty to be commuted. Yet no such reprieve was forthcoming, neither from Sir Nash Grose, the trial Judge, nor the Duke of Portland, the Home-Secretary. It was as if Sarah Lloyd was being punished for crimes other than the one she had been convicted of. What seemed less fair was the fact that Joseph Clark, Sarah's lover, had walked free.

However, a number of things mediated against her. The unwritten bond of trust expected between servant and mistress had been broken. London papers reporting the trial were far less kind than the local press, doubtless affecting the Home-Secretary's opinion regarding the case. Also, Sarah may not have been helped by the somewhat over-zealous attitude of her barrister, Capel Lofft, who turned the case into something of a personal crusade. This had the effect of antagonising both the Judge and the Duke of Portland.

This, like the cases of Margaret Catchpole and William Corder, has been rigorously examined through the years, and there is any amount of information in books and on the Internet. Sarah Lloyd was the first woman to be hanged in Suffolk for fifteen years and drew a large crowd. She was penitent and accompanied by both Mr. Orridge, the prison governor at Bury, and Capel Lofft who delayed the proceedings by speaking at length to the assembled throng.

Sarah's mother hanged herself in despair on hearing of the execution of her daughter. It is not certain what happened to Joseph Clark, her former lover, though it is believed he married in Hadleigh and was buried there in 1835, aged 65.

There is a stone on the charnel house in Bury graveyard bearing the following inscription as a memorial to Sarah Lloyd.

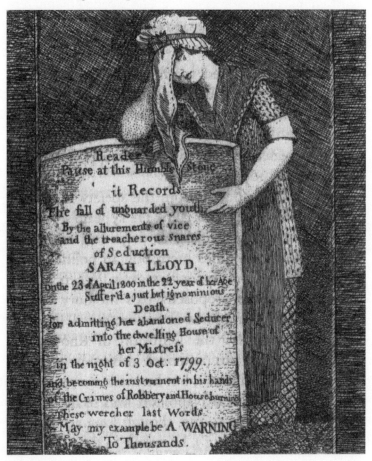

Reader
Pause at this Humble Stone
it Records
The fall of unguarded youth
By the allurements of vice
and the treacherous snares
of Seduction
SARAH LLOYD,
On the 23 of April 1800 in the 22 year of her Age
Suffer'd a just but ignominious
Death,
for admitting her abandoned Seducer
into the dwelling House of
her Mistress
in the night of 3 Oct: 1799.
and becoming the instrument in his hands
of the Crimes of Robbery and House burning
These were her last Words
May my example be A WARNING
To Thousands.

## William Pizzey & Mary Codd ~ Acquitted August 1808

This case is worthy of note, even though it did not result in any kind of death sentence. These two were tried for *"feloniously administering a certain noxious and destructive substance to ANN CHENEY, with intent to produce a miscarriage."* Ann Cheney was 26 and came from Haughley. This was one of many cases of the strengthening of the law around this time to turn what had formerly been a lesser crime into a serious one. In 1803 it had become a capital offence to bring about miscarriage in a pregnant woman.

Confused by conflicting evidence, and worried by the seriousness of the crime, the jury was reluctant to find either of them guilty, and they walked free.

## Shadrach Dewey ~ Hanged April 12th 1806

When Shadrach Dewey shot Captain Thomas Brooke in the parish of St. Mary, Stoke, Ipswich, he loaded his gun with whatever was to hand. As well as the powder, he put in some pebbles and one of his own regimental buttons. Attempting a robbery, he shot Captain Brooke in the jaw. The surgeon, finding the button, it was not long before a number of the 7th Light Dragoons were being questioned by the constables. Dewey was captured, though his associates, Hatcher and Wiggington had disappeared. Dewey alone was charged with *"feloniously and maliciously shooting at Thomas Brooke... with intent to murder, rob or disable him."* (Trial details at Ipswich Record office)

Dewey tried to claim Hatcher had done the shooting, but could not dispute it had been his own gun. The shady world of conscripted soldiers was laid bare here. Ipswich was full of them, from a host of regiments. Many were bounty men, signing up for, then deserting from regiments; hard-drinking men with little respect for law and order. A key witness in this trial was a recaptured deserter named George Favell whose testimony was likely to favour the one who offered him the largest bribe. In the end, Dewey had little chance of avoiding the hangman's noose. *"The unfortunate man seemed prepared... and met his fate with becoming resignation."*

## Luke Castle & Samuel Wheeler ~ Hanged August 27th 1806

At the Summer Assize of 1806, only 12 prisoners appeared on the calendar for trial, but *"so notorious were their offences that the following 8 received sentence of death."* (Ipswich Journal: Aug. 17th) *Luke Castle and Samuel Wheeler (both under 22 years of age) for a burglary in the dwelling house of Mr. John Chapman of*

*Stradishall, and stealing therefrom sundry articles of wearing apparel &c.*

***Henry Deighton***, *for breaking open the dwelling house of Mrs. Ursula Traylin of Great Thurlow, and stealing therefrom a silver watch and many other articles.*

***John*** *and* ***Tho. Hurst*** *(father and son) for stealing one Southdown ewe and one Southdown lamb, the property of Mr. Abraham Constable of Stradishall.*

***Wm. Parsons***, *alias* ***Sparke***, *for stealing a chestnut mare, the property of Mr. John Hayward of Lawshall.*

***Miles Rayner*** *and* ***Wm. Burrell***, *for stealing a bay mare, the property of Mr. Th. Mallows of Ipswich.*

These cases reflected the way the law operated at that time. William Parsons and the two Hursts were reprieved at the end of the Assize by the Judges, Sir James Mansfield & Sir Nash Grose. A reprieve was later obtained for Henry Deighton on the understanding he should be transported for life. Burrell too was reprieved, but his partner in crime, Miles Rayner hanged at Ipswich on August 30th. Rayner's past record had caught up with him. The Ipswich Journal pulled no punches in reporting the justness of the intention to execute the other two sentenced to death.

*The singular and attrocious conduct of Luke Castle and Samuel Wheeler in robbing Mr. Chapman of Stradishall cannot but convince every reader of the justness of their sentence. The villains (who had long infested that neighbourhood, and belonged to a gang of that class denominated Gipsies), at midnight entered the dwelling house of the said Mr. Chapman, who resided therein alone, most cruelly beat and tortured him with a bayonet, in order to extort from him his property, and afterwards attempted to enclose him in a hutch, which not proving of sufficient length, induced them to threaten to shorten him by cutting off his head... They then, before they departed, obliged him to kiss a bible, and swear he had no property but what they had taken, and with shocking imprecations threatened if he attempted to unbind himself before they returned, to murder him.*

Ipswich Journal: August 17th 1806

This being the case, it comes as no surprise that few tears were shed for such a pair of hardened criminals.

### Robert Clarke ~ Hanged April 8th 1807

The Suffolk Record at Ipswich has a document from the time that gives a full biography of Robert Clarke, detailing his descent into crime and his eventual come-uppance. As has been shown, these were frequently published locally and sold for a few pence around the time of the execution.

Clarke had been born in 1767, of respectable parents at Wacton in Norfolk. He had begun in service to a farmer at the age of 12, but at 17 had enlisted with the 68th Regiment of Foot, being sent to Gibraltar. When peace was declared, he was deemed too short to be a regular soldier, so was discharged. Moving to London, he worked as a gardener and as a stable lad. He married in 1790, but soon left his wife and started a number of *'illicit connections with other women'.* It was learning the trade of a house painter that opened his eyes to the possibilities for making a living by thieving. He was in a strong position to study places ripe for robbery. He spent a number of years successfully evading the law, but it was a change of modus-operandum that was to prove his undoing.

Having lived for a while in Norwich, he was finally apprehended for *'uttering a false bank note in order to defraud William Plume.'* When arrested in Bury St. Edmunds, he attempted to throw a parcel over a garden wall. The parcel contained another 54 similar notes. He proved a fairly desperate prisoner, attempting first a gaol break, then feigning madness. Eventually, we are told, he saw the error of his ways and *'found God.'* He received no less than 27 visits from ministers of religion between March 23rd and the day of his hanging a fortnight later.

At the last, he wanted to make a full confession, calling out as he went to the scaffold, *"Tell Mr. C\_\_\_\_ at Norwich, that I was the person who took those things from Col. Woodhouse, but it slipped my mind till now."*

A stone erected over his grave read...

A
## MEMORIAL
OF
# ROBERT CLARKE
Who died April 8th 1807
### AGED 40 YEARS

THE WAGES OF SIN IS DEATH

Reader consider!
Nothing is worth a thought beneath,
But how you may escape the death
That never, never dies:

How make your own election sure,
And, when you fail on earth, secure
A mansion in the skies.

## John Dogharty & Matthew Reilly ~ Hanged July 31st 1809

If ever there was a case that warranted a hanging, this was it. Following a drinking session in the Joiner's Arms in Ipswich, these two drunken Irish soldiers identified a man with money on him, and were prepared to stop at nothing to avail themselves of it. Robert Howe had been a soldier for only a few days, and still had most of the six pounds bounty he had been paid to enlist. By this time, it was worth a good bit more than *'the King's shilling'* to join up. Dogharty and Reilly set about the man with a bayonet, putting out his eye, and stabbing him in the chest, before leaving him for dead. He did not die immediately. Though it was a while before he was found, he had occasional moments of lucidity before he became delirious and died. Constables arresting the two killers found their work was made easier because each man incriminated the other, and their joint testimonies were enough to hang them both. Neither man was more than 22 years old. A large crowd cheered when they hanged.

## Maurice Griffin ~ Hanged March 28th 1814

Most references give Griffin's age as just 17, and if that is true, he was probably the youngest to hang in Suffolk over the last 300 years. However, the court report gives his age as five years older, and this may be more accurate. It all seems to have been another case of a young soldier with too much drink inside him. Quartered at Woodbridge, with the 69th Regiment of Foot, Griffin got into a scuffle with a comrade, Thomas M'Mahon, and determined to settle the matter by fetching a bayonet, with which he killed the other soldier. The jury simply had to decide whether this was an impulsive killing, in which case it was manslaughter; or a more premeditated act, in which case it was murder. The jury decided that as Griffin had gone away from the bar to fetch a weapon, he had thought about it in advance, and that made him a murderer. He was just another soldier, and Suffolk had seen so many of them hanged, imprisoned and transported, little thought was given to his plight. However, some capital cases elicited a bit more public sympathy...

## Ann Arnold ~ Hanged March 29th 1813

The Parishes of Suffolk were full of young girls who were pregnant, and found themselves abandoned by the fathers of their children. Many of these bastards did not survive, their demise often hastened by a desperate mother. Most cases, if they came to court at all, resulted in acquittal. At inquests into such deaths, the Coroner frequently gave the cause as *'overlain'* (accidentally smothered, as mother and child shared a bed). In the case of Ann Arnold, that was not an option. Her child had been found stripped and thrown into a pond at Spexhall...

*One witness deposed that the prisoner had told her "that she had such temptations when she came to the pond, that she could not go backwards or forwards till she had drowned the child." When the prosecution closed and the prisoner was called upon for her defence, she said, "I knew nothing of what I was about till after I had done it." The child, it appeared, was not found till three weeks after the commission of the act by a boy who was keeping sheep in an adjoining field. The case of this unhappy culprit shews, in strong colours, the depravity to which the human mind may be brought, when it has lost its sense of rectitude. From her own acknowledge-ment, the poor babe exclaimed, on being stripped, "Mother, what are you going to do?" Callous, indeed, must that heart have been, when such an appeal could not soften it. It seems she had been delivered about 9 weeks after Michaelmas of a second bastard child; and had flattered herself, that the father of it would marry her, if she could prevail upon the parent of her first child, who allowed 1s.6d. per week for its main-tainance, to take the sole charge of it. This he refused to do; and it is thought the disappointment prompted her to commit the horrible act.*

As was reported on page 29, her sentence was to be hanged and her body dissected. A measure of public sympathy would have no effect on the process of the law.

The trial report describes how the judge *'was so much affected in passing sentence that he could not refrain from tears, but the prisoner appeared but little affected with her awful state.'*

Infanticide was not uncommon. In a similar case that came to trial the following year, **Mary Gibbs** was found guilty of the murder of her two year-old (The trial record says 14 months) bastard child whom she had left on the banks of the River Alde at Hollesley. The child was later found drowned. In her testimony, she commented that she would not have done such a thing, *"had it not been for the blackguard of a father."* The trial judge commented that if this had been the drowning of a bastard baby by a mother *'desperate to hide the shame of her seduction,'* her life might have been spared, but that excuse was denied by the age of a child, he felt, she should have protected at all costs. At her execution, it was reported that *"although only 23 years of age, from intemperance and disease, appeared much emaciated."* The Ipswich Journal reported that she and Maurice Griffin, another criminal who was hanged at the same time, were very penitent and acknowledged the justice of their sentence. It was said, *"they shook hands just before the drop fell and were released from their miseries."*

Many more such killings of children by desperate single mothers must have gone undetected, as large numbers of 'base-born' children never reached their first birthday and these were early days for forensics. Without a mother's confession, it was hard to prove infanticide.

## Elizabeth Woolterton ~ Hanged July 25th 1815

Whilst the death of an infant at the hands of desperate single-mother could be understood, no such mitigation could apply to the case of Elizabeth Woolterton. Living at Denton in Norfolk, she had sent a cake and a piece of veal to her uncle-by-marriage, 83 year-old Tifford Clarke, at Kirby Cane, near Beccles. He claimed Elizabeth owed him money and must have been looking for a way to get out of debt. Also, it was revealed, Elizabeth stood to inherit on her uncle's death. Presumably, when she laced the cake with arsenic, she expected it to be eaten by Mr. Clarke. Unfortunately, it was cut into pieces and given to a number of children, one of whom died. Witnesses testified to the fact she had purchased arsenic, *'to poison vermin'*, only a week earlier. It only took the jury twenty minutes to decide her fate, and although the execution was delayed a day, thirty-six hours after the judge had donned the black cap, she was dead.

Her execution was just one day before one of the most famous arsenic poisoners of all time met her own end at The Old Bailey in London.

Eliza Fenning died, possibly innocent of the crime for which she was convicted. But she, it was said, had poisoned her employer, Mr. Turner, by mixing arsenic in dumplings she made for him. Others suggested that Eliza, a very pretty girl, had been the mistress of her master and this was a way the wronged wife could rid herself of both of them. Eliza protested her innocence to the last, and her story was sold and told across the country for a number of years. (The Ipswich Record Office copy is a 5th edition) It may have proved the incentive for **Catherine Foster** to attempt a similar crime 32 years later.

The next seventeen years would see huge numbers given sentences of death, with no real intention of most of them being carried out.

| Year | Death Sentences | Hanged |
|---|---|---|
| 1816 | 17 | 1 |
| 1817 | 16 | 0 |
| 1818 | 14 | 1 |
| 1819 | 27 | 3 |
| 1820 | 22 | 0 |
| 1821 | 20 | 1 |
| 1822 | 22 | 4 |
| 1823 | 20 | 0 |
| 1824 | 40 | 4 |
| 1825 | 22 | 1 |
| 1826 | 15 | 0 |
| 1827 | 20 | 0 |
| 1828 | 24 | 1 |
| 1829 | 25 | 3 |
| 1830 | 21 | 1 |
| 1831 | 29 | 1 |
| 1832 | 31 | 3 |
| **Totals** | **385** | **24** |

Even as early as 1820, many were saying this was making a mockery of the law. It was widely believed that too many offences carried the death penalty and that the wide discrepancy between death sentences and executions was unacceptable. Capel Lofft, the barrister who had failed to save the life of Sarah Lloyd in 1800, had taken up a number of reformist causes. This was another he would wholeheartedly embrace, as this section of a letter to the editor of the Suffolk Chronicle shows.

...It is but lately, at BURY, at the Assizes, that a respectable *young woman,* at least in behaviour and appearance, was in agonies on sentence of Death being passed on her *brother;* and he, in prison, committed *suicide,* as far as depended upon himself, though unexpectedly discovered and revived. And yet the sentence of death was *not* executed upon him; nor, I believe, *ever meant* to be so from the first. So little, as your *Correspondent* observes, can the *humane* discretion which a Judge can exercise, secure against the worst consequences of *sanguinary laws.* In another instance, at *one* Assize at *Bury, one* young woman *suffered death,* another, for a similar crime, had her life *spared,* who, I believe, said the truth in saying that she *wisht* to *exchange* her fate with her who was left for death. And indeed, *death* is *not,* in many instances, the punishment, the expectation of which is most *dreadful* to the offender. *Discretion* in the *Judges,* extending to *life* or *death,* is a painful trust to the *considerate* and *benevolent:* who know that as systems, opinions, and feelings differ, it may and will betray others into a *false* expectation that *their* lives too will be spared.

And I take it to be far from a fact, that for the *smaller* offences death is *never* inflicted. For some such it *usually* is: and for the *hundreds* (for so many there are) for which it *may,* on the first or *second* delinquency, I know not whether there be *one,* in which it has not been, even within these *few* years, the *actual* result. That it *may be so,* in such cases, is certain. And the *life* of *one* man is too much to be thus left to the doubtful arbitrament of *another.*

He argued that criminals should be able to know what the limits of their punishment might be, and that a tariff be laid down for judges that reflected the seriousness of the crime, on a scale rising as the offence was repeated. The letter was dated March 1818.

Times were a-changing, however, as can be shown in the comparative treatment of two trios of burglars, just ten years apart.

### Joshua Ranson, William Hilyard & Henry Laws
### ~ Hanged April 17th 1819

The jury at the March Assize of 1819 heard a sorry tale of a group of armed robbers who came in disguise to  threaten and rob a wealthy 58 year old widow, protected only by one servant. Probably about five were in the gang, but in spite of their wearing black fur masks, these three were identified and tried.

Sophia Pemble of Whitton near Ipswich and her servant, Susan Hitchcock were threatened at gun-point by Joshua Ranson, who *"said he would blow her brains out if she did not deliver up her keys and her money."* They stayed a while to steal money and a quantity of silver.   It was the silver that proved to be their undoing as they showed it to a number of people in Ipswich, Colchester and Wivenhoe, in an attempt to sell it.   One Moses Ansell, described as a hawker, recalled being offered a number of the stolen objects including some silver tea-spoons and a pair of silver salt shovels.

Finally Constable Bristo was despatched to arrest the three in Colchester and remaining articles in their possession were identified by Mrs. Pemble.

There was some disappointment that the three, as death approached them, were unwilling to confess to any of the other local robberies they were suspected of carrying out.   They did however name their leader, a man called Mayhew, *"who hitherto has absconded."* (Ipswich Journal: April 24th 1819)

Their hanging drew an enormous crowd...

*From a very early hour on Saturday morning, every road leading to this town was thronged with men, women and children, literally treading on each others' heels, and many pressing forward with a degree of zest and eagerness ill suited to the melancholy scene they were about to witness.*
Ipswich Journal: April 24th 1819

Ranson, a baptist from the Stoke parish of Ipswich left three letters for his minister, Rev. Mr. Payne, who read them from the pulpit the following day, *"to warn frequenters of public houses and dissolute companies to desist from such practices."*

## James Peachey, William Alexander and George Leabon ~ Sentenced to death March 1828

Less than ten years later, in a not dissimilar crime, three bad boys from Bacton robbed an elderly auctioneer by the name of Philip Hicks at Wetherden. In typical style, they were operating at least two parishes from where they lived, as they had when robbing the Yaxley Bull a few weeks earlier. Though no firearms were involved, they too came with their faces masked and used a good degree of violence on Mr. Hicks, his wife and their lodger. Discovering the wine cellar, they finally departed with the loot, and a lot of alcohol inside them, as a result of which they were heard going home by a lot of witnesses and it was not too difficult for parish constables to trace them.

At their trial, they chose to plead guilty, in spite of the judge warning them it would do them no favours to do so. They were finally found guilty and donning the black cap...

*The learned Judge, with great solemnity, then proceeded to pass sentence upon them. He said he had appraised them of the awful circumstances in which they were, they had nevertheless after due consideration repeated their plea, and it was therefore his duty to inform them of the consequences which were to follow. The offences were of great magnitude, for in reading over the depositions of the case, he had observed that one of the prosecutors was far advanced in years, was debilitated in ill health, and had not left his bed for many months. One of the prisoners had held a poker over him and threatened to drag him from his bed if he did not tell him where to find his money. [Peachey exclaimed, "that's as false as God is true"] They were a dreadful gang and used masks to conceal their features in pursuing their violent outrages and midnight depredations. It was his duty to pass the awful sentence of the law upon them, leaving them not a hope of mercy. After two sabbaths had intervened, they would be led to an ignominious death, and be ushered into the presence of the Almighty. He therefore recommended them to lose no time in false hopes, but listen to the advice of a minister of our holy religion, and through mercy to implore the forgiveness of their Creator. The sentence he should pass upon them was, that they should be taken to the place from whence they came and from thence to the place of execution and there to be hung by the neck till they were dead, and he hoped that the Lord would have mercy on their souls. Alexander and Leabon were much affected but Peachey walked from the bar with great self-possession.*

Suffolk Chronicle: March 29th 1828

It was about as unambiguous a statement as was ever made in a court of law, leaving the three no hope that their lives would be spared. But this was 1828 and very few would now hang for burglary, however violent. Before he left Bury St. Edmunds, the judge had commuted their sentence to one of transportation for life.

From 1827, courts began to make a distinction between the lesser **'Death Recorded'** and the full **'Sentence of Death'**. For all that, in 1827-8, in addition to 35 who were classed as 'death recorded', eight received sentence of death, but all but one were reprieved. Most were transported.

Convicts on their way to be transported

Only one hanging occurred at that time - William Corder, whose story is told on page 76.

### James Phillips & John Wade ~ Hanged August 14th 1822

Two of a gang arrested for burglary in the Hadleigh Hamlet, these men left wives and a total of 12 children to be looked after at the expense of the parish. They also suffered one of the most botched hangings ever seen in this county.

Along with Charles Norford, Richard Kemball and James Wright, they robbed John Quinton and his family of a quantity of silver and such money as they had in the house. Again, their undoing was the difficulty in selling the stuff without attracting undue attention. An Ipswich watchmaker had been approached but became suspicious and reported to the constables what he knew. Most of the men were easily identified, but Norford could prove he was sleeping with his housekeeper on the night in question and was acquitted. Kemball and Wright were later reprieved and transported to Van Diemen's Land (Tasmania), but the other two were left for execution.

*Wednesday last James Phillips and John Wade, for a burglary at Mr. John Quinton's of the hamlet of Hadleigh, suffered the awful sentence of the law at Bury St. Edmund's. About twelve o'clock, the unfortunate culprits were conducted from the gaol to a field where the drop was erected. When the executioner had adjusted the rope for suspending Wade, the platform, by some extraordinary accident, suddenly gave way, and the unhappy man was soon released from his sufferings, but Phillips was precipitated, with two attendants, to the ground, a circumstance which excited strong feelings of horror among the spectators. After some time, a temporary stage was prepared, and Phillips was launched into eternity, after expressing a hope that his fate might prove a warning to others. An immense concourse of persons were present to witness the awful spectacle, including a number of females!! A general feeling of sympathy pervaded the crowd.*

Suffolk Chronicle: August 17th 1822

## William Aldous & Robert Bennet ~ Separately convicted and hanged April 20th/August 17th 1822

One of the greatest fears at this time was fire. Most towns and villages had a tale to tell of a major disaster whereby a sizeable proportion of their houses had burned down at some point in history. If a fire took hold, little could be done about it until it had run its course. Fires were started deliberately, especially on farms where poorly paid or sacked workers might take their revenge on the farmer responsible for their plight. As a result, arson was sometimes punished with the severest application of the law.

William Aldous, it was reported, set fire to his master's barn at Stradbroke, his reason for doing so being that *"he had never liked his old master"* and had *"set fire to the barn by putting two lighted matches to some straw which appeared through some boards at the back."* (Suffolk Chronicle: August 3rd 1822)

This use of the word *'matches'* is an interesting one, and presumably refers to lighted tapers, as proper *'friction matches'* had not yet been invented.

In the case of Robert Bennett, he set fire to the buildings of Rectory Farm, Mellis, the property of Mr. Robert Downing, using a tinder box and coals from the fire. Though another young man, Robert Gayfor was tried for this offence, he was acquitted.

Both were hanged at Ipswich *'at the drop over the turnkey's lodge.'* Aldous, aged just 17, *"acknowledged the wickedness of the act, and the justice of the punishment. He prayed very earnestly with the Chaplain, just before he ascended the scaffold; and even when he had ascended, he requested to be allowed to say a prayer, when he repeated the Lord's Prayer and after it, the Creed, and died exclaiming, "Lord have mercy upon me - Christ have mercy upon me."* (Suffolk Chronicle: April 27th 1822)

However, things were just about to get a whole lot worse where 'incendiarism' was concerned. John Walker, a pharmacist in Stockton-on-Tees was experimenting with phosphorous, potassium chloride and antimony sulphide in an attempt to create the first friction match, which he did successfully, selling them wrapped in a sheet of sandpaper for striking. But he did not patent his invention, and it was left to a London shopkeeper called Samuel Jones to really put matches on the map. He called them

*Lucifer Matches*, and though his product was superseded by others within a few years, the name stuck, and for a century, all matches were referred to as **'Lucifers'**.

When it needed a tinder box and no small amount of skill to coax a flame into being, arson was much more difficult. Once lucifers became readily available, anyone could set light to things, even small children... and they did! Cases of arson grew throughout the 1820s and 1830s, but even several high-profile trials, followed by public executions failed to halt it. In 1844, there were so many cases of deliberate firing of farm buildings, the trials were referred to as **'The Fiery Assizes.'** Small children as young as 11 were sentenced to transportation, as arson was no longer a capital offence by then. Practically every newspaper in the mid 1840s carried a headline **"Lucifer Matches Again!"**

## Moses Long ~ Sentenced to death April 1823, Death recorded August 1827

It seems incredible that such a pathetic character and totally inept criminal as Moses Long should have attracted not just one, but two death sentences. Nevertheless that is just what happened.

*Moses Long was convicted of a burglary in the house of Mr. John Peck, of Brockford. A curious confession was made by the prisoner; from which it appeared that he entered by breaking a pane of glass, marched about the house throwing open all the doors; lay down upon a bed and slept, he supposed, above an hour; came to another bedroom, and again lay down, but in a few minutes got up again, and "squatted down" upon the stairs; went into the kitchen and cut a candle which he found there. He afterwards took up a parcel of bank notes and laid them down again, thinking them letters; seeing something which looked like a desk, he opened it, and putting his hand upon some black and white stripes - to his great astonishment and terror, a noise proceeded from them, and he ran away as fast as he could. This was a* piano forte! - *The Court was convulsed with laughter at this confession, from which, and other circumstances, it appeared that the prisoner, who was an inmate of the workhouse, was a man of very weak understanding, but capable of distinguishing right from wrong. He was sentenced to death, but reprieved.*

Suffolk Chronicle: April 5th 1823

He was not even sent for transportation this time, but when he attempted to burgle a house in Wickham Skeith in 1827, his second death sentence became one of transportation for life to New South Wales. He had stolen a pair of boots.

### Robert Rule & Edward Green
### ~ Separately sentenced to death in July 1826

Two rather different cases were given much the same treatment. Robert Rule had robbed James Creasy, a somewhat inebriated farmer, as he made his way home to Alpheton, stealing his hat and his pocket-book in March that year. On the other side of Suffolk, at Ufford, Edward Green was busy stealing from the house of Ann Amos in Ufford, near Woodbridge. He took "a seven shilling piece and divers other articles." The owner was able to identify the coin as it had a dent on the face, and it was found wrapped in a handkerchief she had embroidered herself. Both men were found guilty of their respective crimes and sentenced to death. It was specified that Rule would hang at Bury, Green at Ipswich. This was not just a case of '*Death Recorded.*'

The judge explained that under the Act as it now stood, this solemn pronouncement should only be used if it was intended to forfeit their lives. According to an account published of the trial, *"His Lordship said he never pronounced the full sentence without the full conviction that the lives of the individuals must be forfeited."* That may have been his intention, but reprieves were secured for these two, and they, along with four others capitally convicted at that Assize, found themselves on their way to Australia.

## William Corder ~ Hanged August 12th 1828

Corder is undoubtedly the most notorious criminal in the whole county's history. His story has been told in many forms, as as well as acted out in plays and melodramas. Nearly two hundred years have not dampened an enthusiasm for the tale, and his story certainly justifies a place in this book. But it is a story that can be found in so many places, where others are not, so, whilst Corder's crime and punishment are related here, much more detail can more be gathered from a host of contemporary publications, especially the newspapers of the time, national as well as local. This was a story that grabbed the attention of the whole country. The London publisher, Catnach, sold tens of thousands of copies of this ballad.

*Come all you thoughtless young men, a warning take by me,*
*And think upon my unhappy fate to be hanged upon a tree;*
*My name is William Corder, to you I do declare,*
*I courted Maria Marten, most beautiful and fair.*
*I promised I would marry her upon a certain day,*
*Instead of that I was resolved to take her life away.*
*I went into her father's house the 18th day of May,*
*Saying, "My dear Maria, we will fix the wedding day.*
*If you will meet me at the Red Barn, as sure as I have life,*
*I will take you to Ipswich town, and there make you my wife."*

*I then went home and fetched my gun, my pickaxe and my spade,*
*I went into the Red Barn, and there I dug her grave.*
*With heart so light, she thought no harm, to meet me she did go,*
*I murdered her all in the Barn and laid her body low;*
*After the horrid deed was done, she lay weltering in her gore,*
*Her bleeding, mangled body I buried under the Red Barn floor.*

*Now all things being silent, her spirit could not rest,*
*She appeared unto her mother, who suckled her at her breast;*
*For many a long month or more, her mind being sore oppress'd,*
*Neither night nor day she could not take any rest.*

76

*Her mother's mind, being so disturbed,*
            *she dreamt three nights o'er,*
*Her daughter, she lay murdered beneath the Red Barn floor;*
*She sent the father to the barn when he the ground did thrust,*
*And there he found his daughter mingling with the dust.*
*My trial is hard, I could not stand, most woeful was the sight,*
*When her jaw-bone was brought to prove*
            *which pierced my heart quite;*
*Her aged father standing by, likewise his loving wife,*
*And in her grief, her hair she tore, she scarcely could keep life.*
*Adieu, adieu, my loving friends, my glass is almost run,*
*On Monday next will be my last, when I am to be hung;*
*So you young men who do pass by, with pity look on me,*
*For murdering Maria Marten, I was hanged upon the tree.*

The story had all the makings of the perfect Victorian tragedy.
Maria Marten was portrayed as the young innocent girl corrupted

by an older, richer lover, who had murdered her and taken flight. Except she wasn't all that innocent. A veteran of several relationships, she already had a bastard child. She was the daughter of the local mole-catcher. Maria was slightly older than Corder and soon became pregnant with his child, except the infant mysteriously died within a month of its birth. Corder arranged to meet Maria in the Red Barn at Polstead, with a view to their going away together. There it was said he killed her, burying her body under the floor of the barn. Her inquest was unable to establish the exact cause of death as she appeared to have been shot, stabbed and strangled. The likelihood was that Corder's gun killed her. He had dragged the body to her makeshift grave by pulling at the scarf tied around her neck and then used a pick for burying her, which may have inflicted the other wounds. Certainly he always denied using any weapon other than the gun.

Corder made his escape, but continued to write to Maria's parents claiming he was living with her on the Isle of Wight. But his letters all bore London postmarks and suspicions were aroused. Reputedly, Maria's step-mother had a dream whereby she saw the body of her step-daughter in the barn. A search was made and the body found. Corder was found in London, now married, and the murder weapon discovered. After he was found guilty and condemned, although William Corder confessed, doubts always remained about the step-mother's role in the crime.

Corder was the first murderer to be hanged in Suffolk for 13 years and he was always going to draw a large crowd for his execution, but the attendance for this hanging exceeded all expectations.

*From an early hour this morning, the population of the surrounding districts came pouring into Bury; and the whole of the labouring classes in this town struck work for the day, in order that they might have the opportunity of witnessing the execution of this wretched criminal, which was appointed to take place at twelve o'clock at noon. As early as nine o'clock in the morning, upwards of 1000 persons were assembled around the scaffold, in the paddock, on the South side of the gaol; and their numbers kept increasing till twelve o'clock, when they amounted to at least 7000 persons. The majority consisted of men, but we observed a large number of females in the crowd. Two women must have been there at an extremely early hour, for they were close up to the woodwork which surrounded the final drop. They appeared to be of the lowest class; but many of the female spectators were of a much superior grade. Seated on a wall which gave a commanding view of the whole scene, were several ladies dressed in the first style of fashion.*

Suffolk Chronicle: August 16th 1828

The information gathered from four surviving local papers describes how the execution was conducted at the South side of the new gaol in Sicklesmere Road, a special doorway having been cut through the wall to afford access to the scaffold. One of the prisoners had carved *'Corder's Eternal Way'* on the frame.

An early photograph of the front of Bury gaol
(reproduced by kind permission of Bury Record Office - ref: K511/372)

Contemporary accounts go on to describe how the executioner (*"The same one who usually officiated at the Old Bailey"*) clung to Corder's legs, to add his own weight, to accelerate the victim's death. Afterwards, the body was anatomised, wired up to a galvanic battery for experimental purposes, casts made of his features and death-masks created. His skeleton was retained for tuition purposes in the local hospital, and even his skin tanned to cover books. Pieces of the hangman's rope changed hands for a guinea an inch, and his final confession made to the prison governor, Mr. John Orridge, printed and sold. The village of Polstead became a haven for souvenir hunters and by the time the Red Barn burned down some years later, most of its planks had been taken.

Maria Marten's original grave-stone was also chipped away at by collecters, until nothing identifiable remained.

MURDER.

THE RED BARN, AT POLSTEAD.

### George Partridge ~ Hanged April 13th 1829

There was one young man in that immense crowd watching Corder hang who would soon be taking his place. If public hanging was meant to act as a deterrent, it certainly didn't work where George Partridge was concerned. Less than a year later, and just seven miles from Polstead, a nine year-old boy called George Ansell in the village of Milden near Monks Eleigh was found in a field, with his throat cut.

This was a case that placed one of the leading witnesses in an impossible situation. The Reverend Mr. Hallwood had listened to the confession of Partridge on the understanding that he would divulge it to no-one. Faced with the dreadful decision of whether or not the seriousness of the crime invalidated his promise, under pressure from the Coroner, he opted to reveal what had been told to him, on the understanding his testimony should not be reported and would remain a secret only to the court. Some hope! Within 24 hours it was reckoned that everyone within fifteen miles of Bury knew the details of Rev. Hallwood's testimony and belatedly, the Bury Post decided to publish the full transcript. Fortunately, there was plenty of other evidence to corroborate the minister's account and though he was both upset and embarassed by the publicity surrounding his betrayal of a confidence, Rev. Hallwood must have known his evidence alone was not what was pointing Partridge to the gallows.

The victim, George Ansell, in spite of his tender age was described as a farm labourer who had been working in the vicinity of his killer. When the body was found, Partridge was nowhere to be found. About dusk of the same day, when he was discovered at Preston, he had a blood-stained knife and marks were discovered on his slop frock. On instructions of the Magistrate, George Partridge was kept in custody, pending the arrival of the Coroner. All the evidence made available, the Inquest jury were agreed this was a case of murder and George Partridge was sent for trial to Bury Gaol.

It was never made wholly clear why a young man like Partridge should have gone to such an extreme. He said the boy had been cheeky to him and he had lost his temper. He made little attempt to cover his tracks. At his trial, the jury only needed a few minutes to find him guilty of wilful murder.

The Governor of the gaol, Mr. Orridge, was of the opinion that Partridge, whilst "*sullen, rather dull, having a down-look and slow intellect,*" was competent to discern the difference between right and wrong... "*I made no observations leading me to suppose there was either idiocy or lunacy.*"

He appeared to have made a full confession, and that alone was enough to see him hang. But the truth still to be revealed was the fact that George Partidge had already killed one Ansell child a year earlier: Jonas Ansell, who had received a blow on the head and drowned in the village pond. There had been no evidence to tie the crime to anyone but now George Partridge, faced with his own execution, wanted to come clean. In so doing, he implicated two of his neighbours, Elizabeth Phillips and Elizabeth Ward (mother and daughter) to the extent that they were later questioned as accessories to murder, but released.

George Partridge was one of a family of 18 children, a simple-ton, who went to the scaffold before an audience of thousands, *"another victim to licentious indulgence of the passions."* (Bury Post: April 15th & 22nd 1829)

What was expected was penitence, a good confession and a good Christian death. In the case of George Partridge, that was what they got. The same was true in the next case, that of Ambrose Flack. But the same could not be said of the two that followed that. By the 1830s, concerns were being voiced about all forms of execution, and it only added fuel to the flames if there was doubt over the guilt of the hanged man.

## Ambrose Flack ~ Hanged July 25th 1831

Something else the law and the public expected was that prisoners should at least make a fight of it. However cut and dried the case might have been, it was not good form to plead guilty. When Ambrose Flack, a customs boatman admitted shooting his former boss, Edward Osborne, Justice Lyndhurst said, *"Why do you plead guilty? You must not suppose that it will make the slightest difference in your sentence: think well, therefore, before you persevere with that plea."* (Suffolk Chronicle: July 30th 1831)

Though clearly of very low intelligence, *"to the Chaplain's advice, he clearly paid great attention, and, although his notions of religion (for he was extremely illiterate) were previously very vague, he died fully impressed that though his sins were 'red as scarlet,' yet by thorough repentence, they would be 'white as snow.'"* (Suffolk Chronicle: July 30th 1831)

He would be the last to suffer the indignity of dissection, and exposure to public view, before his remains were given to his friends for a burial, without ceremony in St. Clements Churchyard.

## William Twitchett ~ Hanged August 15th 1832

William Twitchett, for a violent burglary at Stradishall Workhouse, was condemned to death. Though he protested his innocence to the last, he was damned by the testimonies of two people. Mrs. Biggs (or Briggs), Mistress of the Workhouse had suffered greatly in the attack, so "her apparel was not merely spotted, but literally dyed with her blood." She knew Twitchett well and was sure of her identification, (though she had been in 'a state of delirium' for some time after the attack). Added to her evidence, his shoeprints matched those left by the departing felon. A number of pieces of circumstantial evidence were also offered. The other testimony was that of Twitchett's partner in crime, an 18 year-old lad by the name of William Gilly. Courts were unhappy convicting merely on the often tainted evidence of associates, but here it seemed to corroborate other evidence, and the jury were in no doubt they had the right man.

No amount of pleading from the Chaplain or his family would persuade Twitchett to own up to the crime. Even Gilly was taken to him and was reported as saying, *"Don't die with that story in your mouth, Billy!"* Twitchett was unmoved to the last. *"The condemned sermon on the Sunday before his execution* (which was conducted by Rev. T. West, the prison chaplain) *moved many of the auditors to tears, but Twitchett remained apparently unaffected."* (Suffolk Chronicle: August 18th 1832)

Even reformist newspapers like the Bury & Norwich Post and the Suffolk Chronicle felt it necessary to justify hanging a man who remained so adamant he was not guilty.

*As it is highly important, for the moral efficacy of the punishment, that no doubt should exist in the minds of the public as to the guilt of this unhappy man, it may be right to bring to their recollection a few of the main points of the evidence. ...It is, we think, quite impossible to come to any other reasonable conclusion than that Twitchett has suffered by a righteous judgement for one of the most ferocious attacks upon a defenceless unresisting woman that we ever remember.*

Bury Post: August 1832

It was reported that he died without a struggle, having addressed the crowd with the words, *"All you that are standing by, take warning! What I am going to suffer for, I am innocent of - The Lord knows it, and I hope the Lord Jesus will receive me."*

William Gilly, his partner in crime, also stuck to his testimony. Found guilty and death recorded against him, he was reprieved on account of his youth (and his evidence?) and transported for 14 years to New South Wales.

Only 5 people would hang in the next 14 years, but Twitchett had started something. Four of those five would hang without an admission of guilt. This was a time of social change and reform of all kinds. More and more, those against hanging found their voice, and weight was added to their argument every time a man went to his death, whilst doubts remained as to his guilt.

### Edward Chalker ~ Hanged March 30th 1835

The convicted murderer, Edward Chalker went to the gallows vehemently protesting his innocence, with the following words...

*"I am not guilty of the crime for which I am going to suffer, nor do I know who did it. It will be found out when I am gone. Be careful, my friends, if ever you should be a witness before the Judge, what you swear to, when a man's life is at stake. I die innocent and at peace with all. Goodbye, God bless you."*

Suffolk Chronicle: April 4th 1835

The same article finished...

*The customary preparations being finished, he was led to the platform, and at a quarter to one, the drop fell. He appeared to suffer greatly, as his struggles were protracted and severe. The horrible spectacle attracted a vast crowd of spectators; men, women and children, and many females were seen carrying their infants in their arms.*

Chalker (sometimes spelt *Chaulker*) was accused along with four other poachers of killing a night ranger on the estate at Hintlesham. Jeremiah Keys, John Clarke, George Jordan and James Payne were all implicated, though it soon became clear that Chalker was the man most likely to be convicted. Entering the estate in search of game, carrying air-guns and bludgeons, the gang had been confronted by two rangers. In the resulting scuffle, Byham Laws Green was beaten to death with his own gun and a pistol that Chalker appeared to have been carrying. Evidence was patchy in this case, and identification was as much about their dog as it was about them. Keys swore to the court he had never been to Hintlesham, and he and the other men were found *'not guilty.'*
In spite of Chalker's continued insistence he had not killed the man, he was the only one that could, with any certainty, be identified, and he alone hanged. For many years after, those in favour of the abolition of hanging would quote this case as being the case where an innocent man was hanged.

### Edmund Thrower ~ Hanged March 23rd 1812
This case is being dealt with out of its chronological order, as it has so much in common with the one that follows it. Both cases were brutal killings that finally led to justice nineteen years after the event. In both cases, it was the confession of a criminal colleague, hoping to avoid prison that led to the discovery of the killer.

In 1793, The Ipswich Journal reported the inquest on two unfortunate murder victims in the following words.

*The Coroner's inquest sat a second time concerning the murder of Thomas Carter and Elizabeth his daughter, the persons said to be murdered at Cratfield in our last* (edition) *but not being able to find out the perpetrators thereof, have adjourned to Monday the 11th day of November. The body of Elizabeth Carter was found in the yard, near the dwelling house with her brains beaten out, apparently by a hatchet. Her father was lying dead on the floor by the fireplace of his house with his skull fractured and his hat and wig nigh cut through.*

Ipswich Journal: November 2nd 1793

Though information was advertised for, when the inquest sat again, it was still not possible to identify who had been responsible for such a violent crime. However, descriptions were issued of two characters, one male, one female, believed to be involved.

*It appears that a man, a stranger, was seen lurking about in different places in the said parish, on Wednesday afternoon and evening of the 16th; that he wore brown hair, plaited and tied up behind with a black ribbon, had on a light coloured long coat, large round flap hat, black or dark waistcoat and breeches and speckled stockings. A person of this description was seen running very fast in the road leading from the house of the deceased not far from it about 9 o'clock that evening (the time it is supposed the murder was committed) toward Cratfield Bell Green. A woman, a stranger, was seen talking with Mr. Carter and his daughter about 6 o'clock in the evening, dressed in a coloured jacket, blue petticoat and black bonnet.*

Ipswich Journal: November 2nd 1793

In spite of the appeal for information, years were to pass before an arrest was made. John Head, a petty thief, admitted in 1812 that he had vital evidence concerning the Cratfield murders.

During the intervening 19 years, John Head had spent much of his time in prison. For seven of those years, he had been incarcerated aboard a prison hulk under sentence of transportation. He claimed to have given a hammer, which he believed to be the murder weapon, to Edmund Thrower. Two other well known felons of their day were implicated but not indicted: William Smith (known as Gipsy Will) and John Saunders who was under sentence of death for cattle stealing in Norwich gaol.

It was a difficult and complicated case with a lot of conflicting evidence. It was hard for judge and jury to know who to believe. Seeing the way the case was going, Thrower tried to convince the court that Head had played a part in the murder. The motive was never established. In the end, John Head received the benefit of the doubt, and Thrower alone suffered the inevitable judgement.

*Prisoner at the bar, you have been tried and convicted by an impartial jury of your country, of a most foul and cruel murder, a murder of an inoffensive poor girl, who gave you no provocation, and who you did not even know; and of her aged father too, in the moment of quietude. The motives which led to that murder are best known to God and your own conscience. Justice, though slow, has at length overtaken you for this great and heinous offence; and you will do well not to flatter yourself with the hope of mercy betwixt this world and the world to come; and therefore it behoves you to make your peace with God before whose awful tribunal you must appear...*

***You will be removed from hence to the place from whence you came and from thence to a place of execution on Monday next, where you will be hanged by the neck until you are dead, and your body afterwards to be delivered to the surgeons for dissection; and the Lord Almighty receive your soul.***

Ipswich Journal: March 28th 1812

The same paper reported his execution in the following words...

*Thrower, having declared his innocence of the murder to the Reverend Mr. Aldrich, and just at the moment before he was turned off, on being pressed by Mr. Johnson, the gaoler, to confess what he knew about the murder as a satisfaction to the public said, "They will never know it." These were the last words he spoke. His body, after being dissected, was interred on Wednesday night in St. Margaret's Churchyard in this town.*

Ipswich Journal: March 28th 1812

## Samuel Brown ~ Convicted of manslaughter July 1835, & transported for life at the age of 78

It may be that this man does not really belong in this book, as it is unclear whether he received a death sentence or not. His story, however, is one of the most remarkable ones in the annals of crime in Suffolk. Samuel Brown (alias Stumpy) came to the Summer Assize in 1835, accused of a murder he had committed years before.

Twenty years earlier, he had served a short gaol sentence for smuggling. In 1817, at Little Bealings, he had confronted his partner James (or William) Ayton, landlord of The Dog at Falkenham Green, who had 'shopped' him to the authorities. A violent argument followed, and Ayton was stabbed to death. At the time, evidence was thin and witnesses not prepared to come forward.

However, in 1834, James Green, a butcher of Woodbridge, had been accused of stealing 30 sheep in one night, and had found himself in gaol, where, fearing the worst, he attempted to cut his own throat. Remembering he had evidence that might give him some bargaining power, Green obtained a King's pardon in return for testifying in the case of this 19 year-old murder.

Samuel Brown, at 78, was tried for murder, but found guilty of manslaughter, the Judge saying in sentencing him that *"he would be sent out of the country to spend the remainder of his life in hard labour upon the public roads - labour as hard as his advanced age would admit. "* Only in very rare cases was anyone over 50 sent to Australia.

Ironically, just 10 months later, James Green, the witness that sent him there joined him, for the crime of stealing and killing a carrier's horse.

## Mary Sheming ~ Hanged January 11th 1845

The same James Green, just mentioned, had a sister named Mary Sheming, who in 1844, was indicted for the murder of her infant grandchild, using arsenic. She protested her innocence to the end and nothing more than circumstantial evidence was produced. If she did not kill the child, who did? It had to be some-one in the family, even the babe's mother. Her husband and eldest son clearly held Mary responsible, as they were in the crowd of eight to ten thousand that filled the streets *"from the prison to the Admiral's Head Inn on one side, and nearly to St. Helen's on the other. "* This in spite of the fact the weather being appalling, the platform, *"black, sepulchral, horrid thing, looming through the thick and dense atmosphere of a wet and chilly day. "*

Though she clung to her claim of innocence to the last, *"at the foot of the gallows clamoured a dozen wretched creatures vending 'The trial and execution of Mary Sheming', before the breath had left her body. All the particulars of the death being printed and sold before the awful event were, of course, sheer falsehoods. In one of these publications, she was stated to have made confession; in another, that all fortitude forsook her; and a third had append-ed to the relation of the circumstances, a mock lamentation in verse, which, as the days of capital punishment are fast waning away, we give as a thing almost become a relic of the past. "*

> *In Suffolk's dark and dreary gaol,*
> *Lamenting there did lie,*
> *A woman named Mary Sheming,*
> *For murder doomed to die.*

*O God receive my guilty soul,*
*In anguish she did cry.*
*Exposed upon the fatal tree,*
*I am condemned to die.*

Ipswich Women's gaol at the time of its closure in 1931, but little-changed
since Mary Sheming's time (reproduced by kind permission of Ipswich
Record Office: ref: B106/2c/3.1  This picture - neg 23/143,
Title page picture - neg 23/136, picture on page 115 - neg 23/139,
picture on page 118 - neg 23/141)

*A woman for a dreadful crime,*
*In London did bewail,*
*Alas! for murder doomed to die,*
*In Suffolk's dreary gaol.*
*This female, aged fifty-one,*
*How awful to unfold,*
*Her dreadful deeds when you but read*
*Will make your blood run cold.*
*Her own grandchild, a smiling babe,*
*This wretch, alas! did slay.*
*Whatever could her mind possess*
*To take its life away.*

*The deadly poison, arsenic,*
*She to the infant gave,*
*And sent that smiling pretty babe*
*Unto its silent grave.*
*But justice close pursued her,*
*And for murder she was tried.*
*In Suffolk's gaol she did lament,*
*And on the scaffold died.*

*January the eleventh*
*Multitudes did flock to see,*
*This aged woman end her days*
*Upon the fatal tree.*
*For the murder of her grandchild,*
*How dreadful to relate,*
*That culprit, Mary Sheming,*
*Met her untimely fate.*

*Oh! Pray now take warning*
*You females great and small,*
*And think how Mary Sheming*
*Of late met her downfall.*
*It has a great sensation caused,*
*For miles the country round.*
*Such crowd was never seen before*
*As was in Ipswich town.*

Suffolk Chronicle: January 18th & 25th 1845

As is only too clear, this paper at least had no further stomach for such exhibitions and went on to report on the behaviour of those that chose to attend. *"The scenes enacted at various public houses in the town during the day were as bad as possible, and in the afternoon, a large party... wended their way though the streets, calling at the top of their voices, 'JACK KETCH! JACK KETCH!' Yet we are told by our rulers and men who make great parade of religion, that an execution is a great moral lesson!"*

Picture of the hanging of Mary Sheming (Copied by kind permission of Ipswich Record Office as is the picture on page 93)

## William Howell ~ Hanged January 25th 1845
## Walter Howell & Israel Shipley ~ Sentenced to death

This was a case that was bound to attract controversy. Long after the jury had demonstrated that, in their opinion, proof beyond reasonable doubt had been established, much of the evidence that had been presented was being drawn into question. Though there was a respite for the younger of the two Howell brothers and his colleague, Israel Shipley, after a lengthy stay of execution, William Howell still hanged. But that did not silence those who were convinced this had been a travesty of justice.

Serious crimes were often first announced accompanied by the offer of a reward. This was no exception. £100 was offered to anyone giving information leading to the arrest of the criminals responsible for the shooting of J. McFadden, a 27 year-old police constable from Mutford, near Lowestoft. He had interrupted a burglary from a barn at Gisleham (confusingly, some papers report this as Gislingham). McFadden had been set to watch the barn, and on accosting three of a gang of five thieves, had been shot.

He was found still alive, but in spite of being *'transported on a tumbril in which was placed a feather bed, and being administered brandy,'* he died from his injuries. The Suffolk Chronicle suggested that a sizeable portion of the reward offered had been paid to Harriet Botwright of Hulver, a leading prosecution witness, who stood to gain handsomely from the conviction of William Howell. She had not come forward as a witness until two months after the murder, and there were those who questioned both her motive for testifying and the accuracy of her recollection of the events she was party to. Not for the first time, the reformist Suffolk Chronicle would be involved in a slanging match with the arch-conservative Ipswich Journal. In the wake of this case, and in an attempt to press for the abolition of hanging, a petition was raised by the *'Society of Friends'*, signed by 3,850 people wishing to see an end to capital punishment. Though public hangings would be done away with after only 5 more in Suffolk, it would still be over a century before the hangman found himself without work to do.

The Howell brothers were well known felons, and much was

A hurried printing for a hanging - one piece of type was upside down

said of their appalling attitude to authority, especially when the drink was in them. A lot of the evidence against them was circumstantial, but opinion in the court weighed heavily against the men. In this case, the words of the dying man were accepted in evidence, helping to identify the three tried and the firer of the fatal shot. McFadden had taken some hours to die and had been quite lucid for much of that time. He was able to give detailed descriptions of what the men had been wearing, and there seemed no reason to discount what he had been able to tell Superintendent Lark before he lapsed into unconsciousness. Even then, the police and judiciary were particularly determined to punish anyone shooting a policeman in the course of his duty.

Bodies of hanged felons were now being buried at the back of the prison. We are told both Mary Sheming's and William Howell's graves were marked by stone tablets bearing their initials, set into the wall close by.

The tomb of the murdered policeman, James McFadden, in Kessingland

churchyard. This fine memorial was erected by the Chief Constable and the East Suffolk Constabulary in his memory.
(photo reproduced by kind permission of Adrian Pye)

## Catherine Foster ~ Hanged April 17th 1847

The poster referred to on page 22 of this book described one of the strangest cases of murder ever to come before a Suffolk court. The description published here is the account published at the time of her trial and offered for sale (exactly as it was printed, warts and all). As has been mentioned, there are shades of Eliza Fenning's celebrated case of 1815.

# A voice from the gaol

Oh! what a horrible place is a gaol - a criminal's condemned cell! many hath passed by the door in the days of innocence, and subsequently been dragged thither as an unwilling visitor.

There hath been quickened in many a heart the undying worm, and there hath arisen in many a one the effable star. Hope hath laid down the treasure, and fear his burthen on the threshold of that place, and beneath its roof hath met all the secrets, and mingled the emotions of the human soul.

The world would fail know my thoughts and reflections while I lay under sentence of death in this dungeon, although it costs me a severe pang I will endeavour to lay before the reader the awful idea of being suddenly plunged from life to eternity by the hand of the executioner. The moral is a terrible one. I thought that while some fond couple were being formed in the bonds of eternal love, or while some father was hailing the birth of his first born. While in a word, millions and millions were supremely happy, joyous and gay, I thought I was the most wretched, miserable being in the world doomed to a fearful death - the death of strangulation - the death of apoplexy - death by a gush of blood to the brain, the tenderest part of the human body: a death that would leave me dangling in the air, while I could not even gratify the natural impulse of holding up my hands to save myself, because those hands would be bound before, and a cord would connect my arms behind me. Oh! heavens, such a death as this for a human being, gifted with the most acute feeling. Death by strangulation, hanging, falling by one's own weight and then the gush of blood through bursting arteries and veins to the

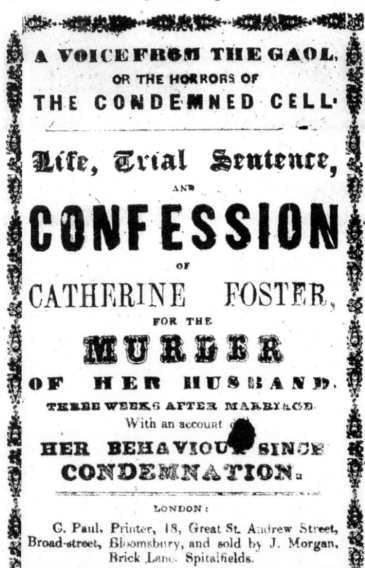

A VOICE FROM THE GAOL,

OR THE HORRORS OF

THE CONDEMNED CELL.

Life, Trial Sentence,

AND

# CONFESSION

OF

CATHERINE FOSTER,

FOR THE

MURDER

OF HER HUSBAND,

THREE WEEKS AFTER MARRIAGE.

With an account of

HER BEHAVIOUR SINCE CONDEMNATION.

LONDON:

G. Paul, Printer, 18, Great St. Andrew Street, Broad-street, Bloomsbury, and sold by J. Morgan, Brick Lane, Spitalfields.

head. Oh! the idea is horrible! most horrible! And then again rushes to my mind those awful moments of once more meeting a tender mother, with my brother and sister in this miserable dungeon, w[h]ere, after a short interview, we shall be separated from the affectionate arms of each other for ever! Oh! how will that dear parent sustain herself under these heavy afflictions, or how shall I be able to imprint the last kiss of my sister, that child who has so often laughed, played, and held out its little darling arms to come to me. Oh! it is the idea that harrows up my soul.

On Saturday, March 27th, at Bury, Catherine Foster was tried for wilfully murdering her husband, John Foster, by mixing arsenic in a dumpling which he partook of. On the prisoner being arraigned at the dock, she evinced but little alarm at the awful position she stood in. The prisoner is described in the calendar as eighteen years of age.

After the whole of the witnesses were examined, the Judge, (Baron Pollock) then recap[i]tulated the evidence with great minuteness to the Jury, who, at half past six retired to consider their verdict, and at ten minutes past seven returned with a verdict of 'Guilty.'

The learned Judge then put on the black cap, and in the most feeling and impressive manner, told the prisoner that she must not entertain any hopes of mercy in this world, as everyone must co[n]cur in the finding of the Jury. He then passed the sentence of death in the usual manner.

The prisoner, who is a good-looking country girl, was then removed from the bar. During the trial, she manifested no excitement, but smiled at her brother while he was giving his evidence.

The facts adduced in support of the prosecution were most extraordinary. The prisoner is the daughter of a decent woman named Morley, living at Acton, a retired village two miles from Long Melford, and three from Sudbury. The deceased, John Foster, was a farmer's labourer, in the employ of Mr. Meeking, at Chitton [Chilton?] Hill, in the vicinity of Acton. They had been acquainted with each other several years, and their marriage took place in the course of last October, and they passed the first week of their honeymoon at her mother's house. The deceased was stated to be a healthy young man, and until the day of his death, had not been scarcely known to have a serious illness. The circumstances of his demise are these:- On the 13th of November, (having been married three weeks to the very day, he returned home about seven o'clock in the evening, in perfect health, and sat down with the prisoner and her brother Thom. Morley, eight years of age, to supper. The meal was of the usual description amongst farmin[g] labourers in that part of the country, consisting of potatoes, dumplings and tea. The prisoner and deceased seemed friendly, at least such is the statement of the boy who was with them. The deceased ate heartyly, but before he had finished supper, he complained of heartburn, and shortly after the things had been cleared away he became quite sick, vomiting continually. The prisoner assisted him into bed, and getting worse, the mother sent the prisoner for 6d of brandy, which she mixed with some oatmeal, and gave it to the deceased. He threw it up immediately, and remarked that he had a burning pain in his inside. During the night he continued in the greatest agony, and at 4 o'clock on the following morning he expired, the medical man who attended him believing that he had died of English Cholera. His sudden demise excited some attention, but no suspicions were entertained that he had been unfairly dealt with, until some fowls belonging to the mother of the prisoner were found dead, after eating something off the dunghill, where the basin in which the deceased had vomited was emptied. It should be observed that at the first post-mortem examination, one of the surgeons declared death to have resulted from the sudden rupture of one of the principal arteries. A difference of oppinion arising however, the authorities of the village communicated with the county officials an exhumation of the body was the result, when it was proved that death resulted from the dreadful affects of ars[e]nic. This circumstance led to the apprehension of the prisoner.

The conviction and condemnation of Catherine Foster, who is only in her 18th year, at the recent assizes, for the Murder of her husband, John Foste, three weeks after marriage, by mixing ars[e]nic in a dumpling which he ate for supper, has produced the most painful astonishment throughout the county, it being generally surmised that the evidence which would be brought against her would be of so conclusive and satisfactory a charactor as that which was adduced at the trial, and which assured her conviction. The motive which could have induced the unfortunate woman to destroy her husband's life so soon after marriage is not as yet correctly traced. He is described to have been a well-disposed and intelligent young man, exceedingly attentive to his home, and devotedly attached to his guilty partner, who, by her prepossessing appearance and engaging manners, had obtained for herself the somewhat flattering title of the "Belle of the Village." (Acton)  A week before the marriage was arranged to take place, she desired to pay a visit to Bury. Here, it seems, her admirer evinced some fears lest he should lose his prize, being aware of her having many would-be lovers; and he earnestly urged her to marriage at once, promising her that she might make the proposed trip to Bury as soon as she pleased after the nuptial

ceremony. Her mother consented to her being immediately united, and the event accordingly took place at the village church at Acton. A week afterwards he allowed her to go to Bury, where it [h]as since been traced, that she lived with her aunt, but where else cannot be ascertained. It is rumoured that she became acquainted with a man, whose name, at present, is unknown. This, in some degree, is confirmed by the observations she was heard to make after her return to her husband, to the effect, that had she gone to Bury before the marriage, s[h]e never would have had him. There was a remarkable piece of evidence excluded by the Chief Baron at the trial. The convic's mother was about dtailing an interview she had with her in the jail. She had the boy, who was the principle witness against the convict with her, who offered his sister a piece of cake, which he was eating. She took it from him, but returned it, at the same time asking him why he told such stories about her to the gentleman at the Coroner's Inquest. Here the mother was stopped by the Baron, on the ground that it could not be received as evidence. Her conduct since her condemnation has been more becoming her awful situation than that which she evinced before trial. Every attention is paid to the spiritual condition of the wretched creature, and daily she is attended by the [R]ev. Mr. West, the chaplain of the jail, the Rev. C.J.P. Eyre, minister of St. Mary's parish; and the Rev. Mr. Otley, of Acton, the clergyman who married her.

The prisoner made a written confession to the Rev. Mr. McIntre, and the Rev. Mr. Otley, on Thursday last, April 1st, but at present we are unable to give any information, as the prisoner desired that it should not be divulged until after her execution.

The unfortunate woman is ordered for execution on Saturday, April 17th.

Catherine Foster pictures reproduced by kind permission
of Bury Record Office: ref: HD1326/1

# COPY OF VEsREs

The solemn knell I think I hear,
Which fills my heart with woe,
For slaying of my husband dear,
I to the grave must go!
Oh! what thousands will approach,
My wretched end to see,
A female eighteen years of age
Upon the gallows tree.

**CHORUS**
Catherine Foster is my name,
Overwhelmed with grief and shame.

My name is Catherine Foster,
Brought up in Bury town,

Respected by my neighbours,
For miles the country round,
I many years might happy lived,
If I had acted right.
But I engaged to wed a man -
Which I could never like.

When 3 short weeks we'd married been
Oh! mark one fatal day,
I strongly was persuaded,
My husband for to slay!
I did some poison purchase
Alas! in Sudbury,
I mixed it in a dumpling
For poor John Foster's tea.

When from his labour, he returned,
His supper was prepared,
And little was he thinking,
That death was him so near.
I beheld him eat the poison'd food,
And I to him drew nigh,
I not one tear of pity shed,
I saw him droop and die.

Come all you pretty maidens,
And shed a tear for me,
a female eighteen years of age,
Doomed to Bury's tree,
I at the sacred alter swore -
To love and to obey,
And three weeks after that I took
My husband's life away.

Now all young men and maidens,
A warning by me take,
Think on poor Catherine Foster,
And her unhappy fate,
If you cannot each other love,
Oh! pray do not be led
Unto the sacred alter -
In wedlock's bands to wed.

My fate is nigh approaching,
The thought does me amaze,
To think I die a death of scorne
At eighteen years of age,
As I John Foster could not love,
I took away his life,
Oh! that I never had agreed
For to become his wife.

It had always been very difficult to diagnose arsenic poisoning. It was readily available for killing vermin, but until the 1830s, its symptoms and after effects appeared similar to those exhibited by a number of common illnesses. Then, a chemist by the name of James Marsh developed what was known as 'The Marsh Test' which was used in a number of high profile prosecutions. By 1847, it was being widely used and though nowhere near as sensitive as modern day techniques, was probably responsible for the rise in successful prosecutions for causing death by poisoning. Just four years after Catherine Foster had been executed, another case of arsenic poisoning would come before a Suffolk Assize, that of Mary Cage, whose tale is recounted on page 105.

## Maria Clarke ~ Sentenced to death, April 1851

*A murder of frightening character was committed on Tuesday evening the 18th (March) at Wingfield, a village two miles north of Stradbrooke near Eye. The perpetrator of the crime*

*is Maria Clarke, aged about 22 years, who made a full
confession. The unfortunate victim is the illegitimate infant of
Clarke aged 6 weeks. The case is rendered more distressing
by the fact that the child was buried alive. It would appear
that a young man named Bowen, residing at Wingfield had
made a promise of marriage; she was apprehensive that if he
knew she had a child he would not perform his promise. She
had no idea of murder until she saw a scuppet standing outside the door and she dug a hole and laid the child in it, she
then sat down and cried, then covered the infant up. She
admitted it when accused, and pointed out to the constable the
spot. Committed to the Assizes.*

Bury & Norwich Post: March 26th 1851

Though attempts were made to show her to be insane, they
were unsuccessful. Her step-father testified that her mother had
been *'thrice inflicted with insanity'* and that Maria had been *"very
odd like her mother."* She was found guilty and a date set for her
execution. A petition was raised, signed by 1,798 petitioners,
requesting her reprieve. In the end fate took a hand. Calcraft, the
executioner, was unable to make the appointed date as he had
similar business elsewhere.

In the meantime, a respite was agreed, though the Bury Post
reported receiving large numbers of letters from would-be hang-
men, volunteering their services to hang the poor girl in Calcraft's
place, some for as little as £20. Maria Clarke was never hanged,
her sentence being commuted to one of life imprisonment. Few
women were to be transported after this point, and never for life.

It is interesting to note that in spite of transportation to
Australia having been in operation for over sixty years, Ipswich
Gaol in 1851 had its highest population of prisoners ever. In
March 1851, when Maria Clarke was arrested, 209 prisoners were
being held in a prison designed for 150.

## Mary Emily Cage ~ Hanged August 19th 1851

At her presentation in court at the Summer Assize, Mary Cage, aged 40, was described as a widow, which was rather ironic as she had been the one to bring that state about.

*Mary Emily Cage was charged with having murdered (her husband) James Cage by administering to him a quantity of deadly poison, called arsenic. The woman who was short in stature was dressed in a coloured faded shawl and black bonnet; there was nothing repulsive in her countenance, which was one of an ordinary description, though a somewhat drowsy appearance gave indications that the prisoner was an opium eater.*

Suffolk Chronicle: August 1851

Arrested just days before the March Assize, the case had been deferred until August. The Cage family of Stonham Aspal were living in what was described as *'distressed circumstances.'* Much of the evidence revolved around the unhappy marriage between Mary and her husband James. She had clearly suffered from his violent outbursts. She had left home on at least two occasions and gone to live with a Robert Fricker. Several of the Cage children were called to testify as to the rapidly declining health of their father, and his final painful demise. It was evident Mary Cage had been slowly administering the poison over a period of time. The chemist who identified it as arsenic was Mr. Image.

It only took the jury twenty-two minutes to weigh the evidence and find her guilty. It was a clear-cut case and no amount of mitigation would save a woman who had gone to such lengths to kill her husband. She had taken pains to purchase the poison several miles away, and appeared to have carefully calculated how best to rid herself of a man she loathed. Much was made of James Cage's suffering and Mary Cage was read *"the sentence of death in the usual form."* At her execution, the Suffolk Chronicle described the watching crowds as *'a seething mass of human beings.'*

*Very few respectably dressed persons were to be seen and most of the houses within view had their blinds drawn down or the shutters closed. The railing around the scaffold was covered to the height of five feet with black drapery, so as to leave only the drop visible. This arrangement, while serving to conceal from the crowd below the appearance of the culprit until the final moment, was well calculated to add to the sombre and repulsive look of the structure... The demeanour of the crowd, with a few exceptions where individuals lighted and smoked their pipes, was on the whole, orderly and decorous. The only instance of heartless brutality was that of a fellow who, the very moment the drop fell, struck up some song of the gallows. He was very properly hooted by those within hearing.*

Suffolk Chronicle: August 1851

Members of the Young Men's Peace League stationed themselves in the various thoroughfares leading to the gaol, and distributed tracts to passers-by entitled: *'A Few Reasons for the Abolition of Capital Punishment.'*

The Cage family would continue to trouble the Constables. After Mary's execution, at least two sons would serve time in gaol and three years later, one (John Cage) would be transported for a serious sexual assault.

Mary Emily Cage was the last woman in Suffolk to hang. But she was far from the only person to be tried for murder that year. In April 1851, at the Spring Assize, six people stood accused of murder, two for manslaughter; also there was a shooting, a stabbing and countless cases of assault. These were violent times. Maria Clarke, as described on page 103 was found guilty of murdering her child at Wingfield, but obtained a reprieve and a prison sentence instead. William Brown, James Sterling and James Cadman walked free from the trial of the murder of a gamekeeper at Elveden. However, in addition to Mary Cage, another murderer was hanged that year.

### George Carnt ~ Hanged April 22nd 1851

George Carnt (or Gant - the Suffolk Chronicle uses both versions in the same article) was to become the last person executed at Bury. After his execution, it was reported that although he left no written confession of his crime, he had made *"frequent and unreserved confessions to Mr. Macintyre, the prison governor and to the prison chaplain, Rev. Chaplin"* He seemed an unlikely killer, the Suffolk Chronicle being of the opinion that he appeared to be a man of *"quite inoffensive disposition, quite incapable of perpetrating a deed of violence."*

It was love story that had gone terribly wrong. Carnt had met up with his girlfriend, Elizabeth Bainbridge, as she returned home from the Harrow public house in Lawshall. She was separated from her husband and living with her brother at the time. The two lovers had exchanged love tokens, she giving him her wedding ring, and accepting his watch in return. It was an exchange they had done before. But this was a relationship that was going nowhere - she was already married. She spoke of her unhappiness and how she wished *"to destroy herself."* Carnt had suggested that if she did, he too would take his own life. Thinking they had a suicide pact, and *"full of beer,"* he set about drowning her in the village pond, before attempting to drown himself, *"but the instinctive love of life prevented him."*

When her body was discovered, George Carnt's hat had been found close by. Her ring was in his purse. She had his watch on a chain round her neck. As a result, he was arrested and charged with her murder. He was described as appearing agitated, saying to someone who offered him a drink, *"This is the last glass I shall drink. The Gallows is my doom!"* He accurately predicted the outcome of his trial. Though an application was made for a remission of the capital punishment, on the grounds *"this was not a killing that came about, as had been surmised, the result of resistance to an attempt upon the chastity of the deceased,"* it was ignored and George Carnt suffered the full penalty of the law.

*We believe that ever since the erection of the gaol, executions have hitherto taken place in the meadow outside the wall, on the South side; and on the occasion of Corder's execution, a door was made in the wall, to avoid the inconvenience of bringing the culprit out of the front entrance through the public road to the scaffold. On the last occasion of capital punishment being inflicted here - that of Catherine Foster - this situation was found objectionable, on account of the nearness of the criminal to the spectators, and the exposure of her figure to the crowd after the drop fell; and it was in consequence determined by the Visiting Justices to stop up the door called 'Corder's Way', and that executions should in future take place on the flat roof between the infirmary on the South side of the entrance and the Porter's Lodge. A new gallows has been prepared, upon an improved principle, by Mr. Darkin of this town, which was not brought out until past seven o'clock in the morning, and by half past eight it was fixed, without noise, almost without driving a nail.*

Suffolk Chronicle: April 26th 1851

In other words, although public hangings would continue a little longer, they were becoming more sensitive about the manner in which such spectacles should now be conducted. On this occasion, about 4,000 attended. The executioner again was Calcraft.

*Shortly after nine o'clock, the death-bell was heard sounding mournfully and the fatal procession began to emerge from the condemned cell... he was conducted to the scaffold, groaning and sighing deeply, and exclaiming in low but audible accents, "Lord! have mercy upon my soul." The rope was adjusted to a staple fixed in the beam, and in less than a minute the cap was drawn over his face, and the executioner*

108

*retired. At the appointed signal, the closing of the chaplain's book, the bolt was drawn, and without a struggle, the unhappy man was dismissed into eternity amidst the breathless silence of the spectators.*

Suffolk Chronicle: April 26th 1851

## William Flack ~ Hanged August 17th 1853

This was, in all probability, a burglary that went wrong. There had been a series of opportunist robberies from houses on Sundays, over a period of about 25 years. These had been carried out in the knowledge that families would be attending church at the time. (See in the appendix: William Matthews, Joseph Read & Thomas Sparks in 1829). In some cases such robberies were from rectories at the time the minister was conducting a service. (See in the appendix: Manister Worts in 1830; Thomas Fletcher & James Rushbrooke in 1834)   This had all the makings of a similar case. Maria Steggles, a servant left behind to cook lunch whilst the rector and his household attended church at St. Mary's, Bacton, was discovered on their return to have been murdered. Her throat had been cut, and she had been bludgeoned. Though still alive when she was discovered, she died almost immediately.

Instantly, a reward of over £200 was offered (half put up by the Rev. Edward Barker, the Rector of Bacton), and a likely suspect quickly arrested.  William Flack had already served time for stealing lead from Bacton church roof.  He was known to be penniless, but after the killing, appeared in local pubs with money to spend. He offered a number of explanations of how he came by the money, but all were found to be false.  His clothes were treated to such forensic examination as was available at that time. Despite a thorough search, the murder weapons were never found. The newspaper reports had little time for this callous killer who smiled as he was led away after being read the death sentence.  He confessed during his time in the condemned cell.   Up till that point, he had given any number of different accounts of his movements and how he had come by objects stolen from the scene.  It was a matter of some concern that they might be hanging the wrong man. Flack's earlier statements made for uncomfortable reading... *"Many of the witnesses have sworn falsely. Many of them have sworn part of the truth, and two of them have not said one word of truth. I am an innocent man."* (Suffolk Chronicle: August 20th 1853) However, as the time drew nigh for his execution, Flack gave a full confession absolving anyone else of the crime. He had knocked at the door of the house expecting there to be no-one there but was confronted by Mrs. Steggles. *"I struck her with my fist. She fell. When down, she cried out violently. I then took a small case-knife belonging to my folks. My little brother called it his. I cut her throat with it, I think, in two places - at least I cut twice. I then knocked her on the head with my boots... I kicked her seven or eight times. I knew she was not quite dead."* He had robbed the house before returning to kick any remaining life out of her. It was a chilling confession and few would feel sorry to see him hang. It was normal by then for there to be a delay of up to three weeks, before execution, allowing time for any representations to be made on the prisoner's behalf. In the case of William Flack, there was to be no reprieve.

## Ebenezer Cherrington ~ Hanged August 17th 1858

When Susan Studd, aged 47, the wife of a baker living near the church of St. Mary Elms in Ipswich, was found by her children, beaten to death, a seedy tale unravelled. Ebenezer Cherrington, it appeared, had worked for Henry Rolve Studd in his bakery since his youth, but had been sacked more than once. He had lived with the family at certain times, and had more than a passing friendship with the baker's wife. The defence tried to portray him as an innocent young man, corrupted by the lusts of an older woman. Henry Studd, her husband, seems to have taken the least line of resistance. When asked why he had not been home that night, he explained that he had bedded down in the bake-house because, *"I heard during the day that the prisoner had been to the house, and I thought if I went home, we might have some words."*

Cherrington had formerly been gaoled for assaulting Mr. Studd.

When a child arrived at the bake-house to inform him his wife was badly injured, he hurried back to find a scene of devastation. There had clearly been quite a fight. Constables were dispatched to Walton, the home of Cherrington's parents, which is where he was arrested.

In his defence, Cherrington said Mrs. Studd had attacked him first with a poker. He had the bruises to prove it. Wrenching the poker from her grasp and fuelled by drink, he had beaten her with her own weapon. *"The prisoner appeared to remain throughout the trial in a state of mental distress."* It was hard to see how this could have been interpreted as a premeditated case of murder. In spite of it all, pleas for mercy and attempts to obtain a reprieve failed. Ebenezer Cherrington was executed *"on a scaffold erected between the 2 turrets at the entrance to the gaol fronting Orchard Street."*

Horrified, in a long editorial, the Suffolk Chronical began with these words...

> *Ipswich has again witnessed one of those demoralising spectacles - a public execution, a mode of punishment, a remnant of feudal barbarism, of which this boasting Christian country ought to be heartily ashamed... It really is high time this relic of a barbarous age were discountenanced. It is a system of legalized murder which is neither required by the decrees of God, nor the exigencies of man.*
>
> Suffolk Chronicle: August 21st 1858

## John Ducker ~ Hanged April 14th 1863

John Ducker, at the age of 63, would become the last criminal in Suffolk to be publicly hanged. The law changed in 1868, requiring all executions after that point to be held in private, within the confines of the prison.

This was a case not unlike that of William Howell in that it resulted in the death of a police constable on duty. On the night of November 25th 1862, a young policeman called Ebenezer Tye, at

Halesworth, was instructed to keep watch over the house of John Ducker, *"as it was then he was believed to carry out his depredations."* Ducker had a long history of criminal behaviour. Later the next morning, the beaten and drowned body of the constable was found face down... *"in a foul stream that all the local privies ran into."*

There was little doubt who was the culprit. When the Halesworth police found him, Ducker's clothes were muddy and wet, and stank of the same stream. He had bruises, as if he had been in a fight. His fate was sealed. Though it was a hanging watched by large numbers, already the sensitivities disturbed by such an event were being attended to, and really it was far less public than many in the crowd had hoped. *"A long black blind partially obscured the prisoner's body from view."*

(Suffolk Chronicle: April 18th 1863)

## James Rutterford ~ Sentenced to death, April 1870

James Rutterford's story was to become legend. Like John Lee, the Torquay murderer, fifteen years later, he was to become 'the man they couldn't hang.'

Poaching was endemic in Suffolk. It was especially rife on the larger estates where pheasants were bred in large numbers. At the very close of the year in 1869, two Breckland poachers, James Rutterford and David Heffer set out with the intention of taking game from the estate of the Maharajah Dhuleep Singh at Elveden. In the nearby parish of Eriswell, they were discovered by 18 year-old gamekeeper, John Hight. In the ensuing confrontation, Rutterford beat the young man to death with the barrel of a gun.

His body was not discovered for 24 hours, but it needed few enquiries to reveal who the likely poachers were. Everyone locally was horrified by the murder. Rutterford and Heffer were arrested and invited to testify at the inquest. Heffer took the opportunity to distance himself from the murder, and turned Queen's evidence. As a result, he was released and served as the main witness for the prosecution at his friend's trial.

Rutterford was sentenced to death and was expected to become the first person executed in private in Suffolk. As the trial judge said...

> *"You must prepare to follow your victim into the other world. I trust you will pay attention to that religious instruction which you will now receive, for only so can you expect to meet your Maker with any degree of tranquillity, resignation or hope."*
> Bury Free Press: April 9th 1870

Hanging ballads were still in fashion, but they could now have a different edge to them...

> *Now these two men do lay in gaol, and bitterly they do bewail,*
> *And Rutterford he cannot fail to look forward to his doom.*
> *But those cursed game laws has been the cause*
> *Of many a life's blood to be shed,*
> *And a warning voice comes from the dead*
> *Saying, repeal the laws, or live in dread,*
> *Of the great Judgement day.*

Public executions had ended in 1867. At this time, the anti-hanging lobby had grown in strength, encouraged by this change. It is not clear how much pressure they exerted in the case of James Rutterford, but the doctors and the hangman came to a strange decision. Just 36 hours before he was due to hang, it was announced that it would be *'unsafe'* to go ahead with the execution as Rutterford had a malformed neck which meant there would be... *"great difficulty in hanging him without risk of failure or prolonged suffering."*

James Rutterford spent the rest of his life in Pentonville prison. This was not a popular decision with most people in the area. David Heffer, the accomplice who testified against him, left the county.

Once hangings were held in private, increasingly few witnesses were invited to be present. It is interesting to note that in the following case, even the press were excluded.

# Henry Bedingfield ~ Hanged December 3rd 1879

The Bury Free Press report of Bedingfield's execution demonstrates how much more subdued reports had become.

*EXECUTION OF BEDINGFIELD - Henry Bedingfield, who was convicted of the murder of Mrs. Eliza Rudd, on the 8th July last, was executed at Ipswich on Wednesday. Many persons expected that a reprieve would have been sent, but the efforts made to that end were unavailable. The black flag was hoisted at eight o'clock, about 300 persons having assembled outside the prison. The representatives of the press were excluded. Bedingfield made no confession, but up to the last charged the crime upon the woman (herself). Marwood was the executioner. An inquest was held on the body at twelve o'clock, before the borough coroner. Bedingfield took a final farewell of his wife on Tuesday afternoon. During the interview, which lasted about an hour, the condemned man protested his innocence of the murder, as he had done all along. He was not guilty, he said, and in the course of time, it would come out who put the razor near his hand, where it was found by the police. His wife informed him of the efforts which had been made to obtain a reprieve. In an interview with the Rev. S. Garratt on Tuesday evening, Bedingfield expressed great fear of the results which might follow his violent end, in the case of his aged parents, whose last surviving child he was.*

Bury Free Press: December 6th 1879

This had been a trial held at Norwich as this Assize served two counties. Bedingfield, along with other prisoners, had been conveyed to and from Norwich by train. A *'stone pavior'* by trade, he was accused of cutting the throat of his lover, Eliza Rudd, (aged 45), before attempting to do the same to himself. Though he continued to assert Mrs. Rudd had committed suicide, expert opinion stated that she would have needed to have been left handed to have cut her own throat in the way she was found.

Unfortunately for Bedingfield, she was right-handed.

This was the first private execution in Suffolk, though quite a large crowd of invited guests still attended the hanging.

### Thomas Lyons Day ~ Hanged November 13th 1883

This was another case tried at Norwich, and large numbers came to the railway stations along the route to get a glimpse of the defendant. It was another seedy tale.

Tom Day killed Lillian Alice Lyons Meek, his child by a girlfriend, Caroline Woodgate, with whom he had a stormy relationship. At the time of the murder, she was married to William Woodgate, of 24, Station Road, Stoke, Ipswich.

Thomas Day knew her as Carrie. Their relationship had been an on-off one and at times a violent one. The motive for the murder appeared to be his way of getting even with a girlfriend that had spurned him. There was little sympathy from the public at large, though the usual anti-hanging letters were published in the local press.

The gateway to Ipswich gaol

115

In the absence of a murderer to gaup at, the centre of attention became *"the newly appointed public executioner, Bartholemew Binns, who took up quarters at the Mitre Tavern."* His work done, *"Binns took his money and left. At the station, curiosity was again excited, for the idea got abroad that Her Majesty's Executioner was in a third class carriage, bound for Peterborough."*

(Suffolk Chronicle: November 17th 1883)

## George Nunn ~ Hanged November 21st 1899

On the evening of July 8th 1899, Mrs. Eliza Dixon, a young married woman and mother of six children walked across the green at Wortham to the Dolphin, in search of her husband's

George Nunn

supper beer. Eighteen year-old George Nunn, who had been playing ten-pins at the back fancied his chances, and insisted she had a drink with him. After that, she left the pub, taking with her the jug of beer she had come for. When she had not arrived home much later in the evening, her husband began a search. Mrs Dixon was found at two o'clock in the morning with her throat cut.

The Superintendent of Police for the Eye Division, Mr. Page conducted an inquiry which led him to suspect Nunn. He was questioned, and his home searched. Recently washed clothing and a long-bladed pocket knife were sent for examination by a Home-Office analyst. At all interviews, he insisted another boy, Frederick Churchard, had been present, though no charges were brought against Churchard. Nunn was taken to Eye lock-up where, at the suggestion of his father, he confessed to the murder. He had offered the woman money for her favours, and being rejected, had killed her.

Although there had been a local inquest, followed by a burial, it became necessary to exhume Mrs. Dixon's body for the Home-Office doctor to make his examination. George Nunn remained at Eye until his trial. Then...

*PRISONER'S ARRIVAL AT IPSWICH*
*The condemned youth was brought to Ipswich by the train arriving at 7:50. He travelled in a third-class carriage, with drawn blinds, accompanied by two warders. On alighting from the carriage at Ipswich, a crowd who had assembled, in anticipation of getting a glimpse of the prisoner, loudly hooted him as he was hurried to a cab awaiting outside the station. As the conveyance drove away to the Gaol, the hooting was continued.*

Suffolk Chronicle: November 3rd 1899

...and they even had to change trains at Stowmarket.

The jury found him guilty, but made a strong recommendation to mercy on account of George Nunn's youth. Theirs had been an easy task. He was guilty by his own confession, as well as by the weight of evidence, and it took them just 15 minutes to reach their verdict. The judge was less considerate. He announced, *"if young men of 18 commit these horrible crimes out of revenge because respectable married women do not gratify their passions, they must expect to suffer for it."*

There would be no mercy for George Nunn. Under the new 1898 regulations, the execution would be an even more private affair, *"none but those legally entitled to be present being admitted."*

*Outside the gaol, considerable public interest was evinced in the proceedings. In Grimwade St., St. Helens, opposite the County Police Station, and in Bond Street, a large number of people assembled, mostly workmen and boys, the crowd in the latter street, where the best view of the flagstaff could be*

117

Inside Ipswich Men's prison before its demolition in 1931

*obtained, numbering several hundred. At four minutes to eight o'clock, a warder was seen on the roof on which the flagstaff is erected, and from that moment, his every movement was narrowly watched by the spectators, who could just hear the sound of the prison bell which began to toll shortly before eight o'clock. It was, however, four minutes past eight o'clock before the black symbol that the sentence of the law had been duly executed was hoisted amidst cries of 'there it goes.'* Suffolk Chronicle: November 24th 1899

It was further announced that a statement of the execution was posted on the pillar beside the prison gate. The executioner had been (probably James) Billington.

The reason for the crowd gathering in Bond Street was because of the belief that this being the nearest point to the *'execution shed'* it could be possible to hear any sounds that might be forthcoming.

As was the way by this time, the final event would be an inquest on the body of the hanged man. The inquest jury's verdict was that *"George Nunn met with his death in accordance with the law of the realm."*

## Twentieth Century Death Sentences

Though these fall outside the time covered by this book, there is a little detail that is worthy of note. In the twentieth century, in this country, hanging continued for murder until as late as 1960, though there had been several attempts by the House of Commons to abolish it before that.

In total, 1,485 death sentences were passed in Britain in the twentieth century, 763 being hanged (748 men & 15 women). Only three murderers hanged at Ipswich after 1900. These were...

### Arthur Garrod ~ Hanged June 20th 1911

This was an unpleasant tale where a 49 year-old Ipswich man murdered his girlfriend, Sarah Chilvers by battering her to death and cutting her throat. Known locally as *'Soldier Garrod,'* the prisoner attracted a lot of sympathy. His girlfriend had been married twice, and on the day of her death, had been drinking in the Half Moon with another man. After his attack on her, Garrod was reported as saying, *"She's as dead as a rat. I done it. And I wish I was dead too."* Though the jury recommended mercy, and it was hard to see this as a planned murder, he still hanged. Just before his execution, Arthur Garrod was visited in his cell by the Bishop of Norwich.

**Frederick Storey ~ Hanged June 16th 1920**

This was another case of a middle-aged man battering his girlfriend to death with a hammer. An Ipswich tram driver, Storey was tried and found guilty of murdering Sarah Jane Howard at the Maidenhall allotments, near Ipswich. As she was heavily pregnant at the time, this was viewed as a double murder. The court were not impressed with the fact that he was a married man, carrying on with another woman, though his wife did testify for the defence, saying, *"he was always a true and faithful husband."* The full weight of the judiciary was used in this case. The famous Home Office pathologist, Sir Bernard Spillsbury, gave evidence for the Crown. It took just 15 minutes for the jury to find him guilty of wilful murder. In their account of the execution, the Suffolk Chronicle included the information, *"he was left hanging for an hour, according to the rules of the prison."*

**Fred Southgate ~ Hanged November 27th 1924**

It is a bit of a mystery why this last hanging at Ipswich happened there and not in Essex where both crime and trial happened. Fred Southgate, a farm labourer, was tried at Chelmsford for the murder of his wife at Ardleigh near Colchester. He was separated from his wife, Elizabeth, with whom he had led a *'cat and dog life.'* On this occasion, he had gone to her house and after a short conversation, had stabbed her. Though the jury, in finding him guilty, recommended mercy, opinion was that as he had recently purchased the knife, it was a premeditated act, and he became the last person to hang in Suffolk.

Amongst those not to suffer hanging, were a few others who were capitally indicted, or might have been had they survived to plead.

Twenty year-old **Kate Ellen Hanton**, an unmarried mother of Finningham, in 1902, killed her son William at Westhorpe. Though she admitted guilt, there were pleas for mercy from all corners, which were upheld, and she served life imprisonment.

The same year, **William Gardiner** was tried twice for the murder of Rose Harsant at Peasenhall. On both occasions, the jury were unable to agree. This case has been written about and examined countless times. Gardiner was never tried a third time, and moved away to London with his wife, where he died in 1941. Nobody else was ever arrested for the crime.

**Louisa Pearce** was another Suffolk mother to be convicted of murdering her child. This time, in 1906 in Heveningham. The trial was held in January the following year. She was found guilty, but the jury recommended mercy be shown. Her death sentence was afterward commuted to life imprisonment.

In July 1913, following a judicial hearing in Lowestoft, to examine **Louis Thain**'s cruel treatment of his wife, a separation was agreed. His response was to attack his wife and certain unfortunate bystanders. In the melee, a fisherman named Arthur Myhill was shot dead, trying to protect those that Thain was really targetting. Rather than face arrest and trial, Thain shot himself dead.

In a truly strange case, in 1918, **Leonard Sitch**, a baker from Stowmarket, his mind apparently disturbed by people accusing him of being a German, killed his wife and two children, before hanging himself.

In what very nearly turned out to be a double murder in March 1920, **Alfred Youngman**, a bricklayer from Needham Market, besotted by the daughter of a Wickham Skeith farmer, Mr. Reeve, shot and wounded the girl and her mother, before turning the gun on himself.

On December 8th 1929, two poachers, George and Ernest Whistlecraft were arrested for the shooting to death of Charles Cornwell, a gamekeeper, in Stubbly Wood at Botesdale. **George 'Joe' Whistlecraft** was remanded for trial. He denied the charge. Without legal aid (not available at the time to those facing trial for a capital offence), he was nevertheless acquitted. The trial collapsed on two counts. First, the dying victim's damning words were not admissable as evidence. Then, it was shown that the only gun in Whistlecraft's possession at the time of his arrest could not have fired the fatal shot.

## In Conclusion

Over the hundreds of years during which Suffolk courts exercised the power of life and death over those appearing there, it is certain there were miscarriages of justice. Crimes were carelessly investigated, those accused poorly represented, and many found guilty of murder were either insane or desperate and acting on impulse. Wherever the truth may lie, all these cases make good reading, as they have done for the last three hundred years. Our local papers have seen to that. And the more entertaining and bizarre the story, the better. This is a report of the case of **Jonathan Vincent**, tried for murder in 1769.

*On Vincent's tryal it appeared that he removed last Michaelmas from Kelsale to a small farm at Laxfield, where he had left a widow and three children; that the girl he had the child by was his servant at Kelsale, and being dismissed from her place on account of her pregnancy, was supported in a great measure by her friends, he allowing her at the same time a 1s a week; that after a few payments he complained of the expense, and wanted to take the child from the mother which she refused; and that at length, his wife being ill and wanting an assistant, he consented to take both of them to his house, where he inhumanly murdered the infant, by giving it a violent blow on the head, in the absence of the mother, who is about 18 years of age, and the child was 30 weeks old.*

*He told the clergyman who attended him in prison that he was not guilty of the murder; but acknowledged that his avaricious disposition had induced him to oppress people to whom he lent small sums of money. At the gallows he talked to his son about farming business... totally regardless of a future state and persisted in his innocence to the last.*

*It is remarkable, that the day before his execution, he sent for a carpenter to make him a coffin, and being told the price, he said he would not give so much by 3s; and that at Bury he refused to pay his attorney and also for the bed he hired in that gaol, acknowledging that his children might want what money he left, which is supposed to amount to 4 or 500L.*

*Vincent suffered here yesterday in pursuance of his sentence, and his body was given to Mr. Clubbe, surgeon for dissection.*

Ipswich Journal: July 22nd 1769

It is the local papers of Suffolk and Norfolk that have supplied most of the information presented here, and whilst it has always been their pupose to entertain, it is believed that they have been a relatively reliable source of historical evidence. It would be more convenient if the court lists that still survive, enabling us to examine in detail a few years, had survived in larger numbers, or even

---

**BURY ASSIZES,** *Aug.* 9, *&c.* 1753.

Receiv'd SENTENCE of DEATH : JOHN WATLING, for breaking into the Dwelling-House of Mr. *Mott,* Attorney at Law, at *Carleton* ; JOHN WOODS, for robbing Mr. *Ferguson* of *Woodbridge* on the Highway ; WILLIAM MANN, for stealing 34 Sheep from Mr. *Mast* and Mr. *Crane* ; and JOHN KENT, for breaking into the House of Mr. *Francis* of *Kessingland.* Watling and Woods are to be EXECUTED at *Ipswich* ; but Mann and Kent are REPRIEVED.

Order'd to be TRANSPORTED for *fourteen Years* ; SAMUEL HILL, THOMAS HILL, and GEO. KEMP, who were convicted the last Assizes : And for *seven Years,* WILLIAM MOOR, for breaking into the House of Mr. *Cooper* of *East-Bergholt.*

ROBERT STUDD, charg'd with stealing a Gelding from Mr. *Richer* of *Grundisburgh,* is continued in Goal 'till the next Assizes.

John Sheppard, Esq; and Mr. John Jenkinson, were indicted for the Murder of ——— Martin, an Ash Gatherer, at Sweffling ; and the Grand Jury found the Bill : But they did not appear to take their Tryals.

that the newspaper reports had been as complete and as clear as the Ipswich Journal detail from 1753 pictured on the previous page.

The thousand or so names at the back of this book are part of the history of Suffolk, many of whom are long forgotten. Yes, the names of William Corder, Margaret Catchpole and Sarah Lloyd are well documented. But it has been my intention in this book to search the stories of others less familiar. Mostly these are tales of people at the very bottom of the social scale, whose pathetic lives led them to commit crimes that in their day put their very existence in the balance. These were our ancestors, as were the thousands that attended the hangings and sang the execution songs as *'Jack Ketch's victims danced.'* It is easy to condemn their heartlessness, even their unhealthy curiosity, but doubtless, if we had been there then, we would probably have joined them. Who knows, we might even have taken the children and made a day of it.

## SCENE AT IPSWICH ASSIZES

Suffolk Chronicle: January 25th 1907

# INDEX OF NAMES OF FELONS DETAILED IN THIS BOOK

| Name | | Date | Place | Page |
|---|---|---|---|---|
| William | Aldous | 1822 | Stradbroke | 14, 72 |
| William | Alexander | 1828 | Bacton | 69 |
| Ann | Arnold | 1812 | Spexhall | 29, 63 |
| Ellis | Backler | 1900 | Haverhill | 7 |
| Margery | Beddingfield | 1763 | Sternfield | 15 |
| Henry | Bedingfield | 1879 | Ipswich | 114 |
| Robert | Bennett | 1822 | Mellis | 72 |
| Thomas | Bird | 1784 | Ashbocking | 25 |
| Isaac | Blomfield | 1787 | | 28 |
| Charles | Blyth | 1795 | Coddenham | 51 |
| Joseph | Bredfield | 1817 | Eye | 13 |
| John | Britt | 1736 | Capel, near Butley | 19 |
| John | Brook | 1766 | Thorndon | 21 |
| Samuel | Brown | 1835 | Woodbridge | 88 |
| Elizabeth | Burroughs | 1766 | Bury St. Edmunds | 42 |
| Mary Emily | Cage | 1851 | Stonham Aspal | 37, 105 |
| John | Carbold | 1750 | Hopton-on-sea | 21 |
| *Robert* | *Carlton* | *1742* | *Norfolk* | *10* |
| George | Carnt | 1851 | Lawshall | 37, 107 |
| John | Carter | 1779 | | 11 |
| Thomas | Carty | 1785 | Yoxford | 33 |
| Luke | Castle | 1806 | Stradishall | 58 |
| Robert | Caston | 1735 | Ipswich | 25 |
| Margaret | Catchpole | 1797, 1800 | Ipswich | 51 |
| Edward | Chalker | 1835 | Ipswich | 84 |
| George | Chandler | 1736 | Ipswich | 29 |
| Ebenezer | Cherrington | 1858 | Ipswich | 110 |
| Maria | Clarke | 1851 | Wingfield | 103 |
| Thomas | Clarke | 1785 | Yoxford | 33 |
| Robert | Clarke | 1807 | Bury St. Edmunds | 60 |
| Mary | Codd | 1808 | Haughley | 57 |
| Arundel | Coke | 1721 | Bury St. Edmunds | 15 |
| William | Corder | 1828 | Polstead | 31, 76 |
| John | Deane | 1785 | Yoxford | 33 |
| Shadrach | Dewey | 1806 | Ipswich | 58 |
| John | Doe | 1750 | Stowmarket | 21 |
| John | Dogharty | 1809 | Ipswich | 62 |

| Name | | Date | Place | Page |
|------|------|------|-------|------|
| James | Dosser | 1795 | Woodbridge | 51 |
| John | Dowsing | 1789 | Halesworth | 49 |
| Charles | Drew | 1740 | Long Melford | 14 |
| John | Ducker | 1863 | Halesworth | 111 |
| *John* | *Duff* | *1777* | *Ireland* | *39* |
| *Eliza* | *Fenning* | *1815* | *London* | *65* |
| Ambrose | Flack | 1831 | Ipswich | 82 |
| William | Flack | 1853 | Bacton | 109 |
| Catherine | Foster | 1847 | Acton | 22, 95 |
| John | Francis | 1766 | Thorndon | 21 |
| Simon | Frost | 1832 | Nowton | 24 |
| William | Gardiner | 1902 | Peasenhall | 121 |
| Arthur | Garrod | 1911 | Ipswich | 119 |
| Charles | Gawen | 1750 | Beccles | 21 |
| William | Gibbs | 1802 | Kesgrave | 28 |
| Mary | Gibbs | 1814 | Hollesley | 64 |
| Tobias | Gill | 1750 | Blythburgh | 9 |
| William | Godbold | 1784 | | 25 |
| William | Gowen | 1787 | Laxfield | 28 |
| Edward | Green | 1826 | Melton | 75 |
| Maurice | Griffin | 1814 | Woodbridge | 14, 62 |
| Kate Ellen | Hanton | 1902 | Westhorpe | 120 |
| Thomas | Hedgson | 1787 | | 28 |
| William | Hilyard | 1819 | Whitton | 67 |
| William | Holmes | 1805 | Melton | 28 |
| Walter | Howell | 1844 | Gisleham | 92 |
| William | Howell | 1844 | Gisleham | 24, 92 |
| Robert | Hoy | 1779 | Brantham | 42 |
| George | Jackson | 1831 | Bury St. Edmunds | 14 |
| George | Jessup | 1826 | Rickinghall | 14 |
| Henry | Laws | 1819 | Whitton | 67 |
| William | Lay | 1779 | Ipswich | 42 |
| George | Leabon | 1828 | Bacton | 69 |
| Sarah | Lloyd | 1800 | Hadleigh | 15, 55 |
| Moses | Long | 1823, 1827 | Brockford & Wickham Skeith | 74 |
| Thomas | Lyons Day | 1883 | Ipswich | 115 |
| William | Maddox (alias Bolton) | 1773 | Thwaite | 25 |
| Daniel | Malden | 1736 | Ipswich | 20 |
| James | Mann | 1792 | Wickham Market | 11 |

| Name | | Date | Place | Page |
|------|------|------|-------|------|
| James | May (alias Folkes) | 1783 | Eriswell | 43 |
| George | Mayes | 1808 | Thornham Magna | 13 |
| William | Mayhew | 1789 | Brent Eleigh | 48 |
| James | Monaghan | 1731 | Ireland | 31 |
| John | Nichols | 1794 | Fakenham Magna | 50 |
| Nathan | Nichols | 1794 | Fakenham Magna | 50 |
| George | Nunn | 1899 | Wortham | 116 |
| George | Partridge | 1829 | Milden near Monks Eleigh | 80 |
| James | Peachey | 1828 | Bacton | 69 |
| Louisa | Pearce | 1906 | Heveningham | 121 |
| James | Phillips | 1822 | Hadleigh | 71 |
| William | Pizzey | 1808 | Haughley | 57 |
| James | Pleasants | 1816 | Lawshall | 14 |
| | Press Gang | 1779 | Ipswich | 18 |
| Joshua | Ranson | 1819 | Whitton | 67 |
| *Charles* | *Ray* | *1731* | *London* | *31* |
| Matthew | Reilly | 1809 | Ipswich | 62 |
| Richard | Ringe | 1763 | Sternfield | 15 |
| Robert | Rule | 1826 | Alpheton | 75 |
| James | Rutterford | 1870 | Eriswell | 112 |
| *John* | *Rye* | *1777* | *Norfolk* | *30* |
| Jonathan | Sawyer (alias Lock) | 1780 | Cretingham & Brundish | 5 |
| William | Sell | 1779 | | 11 |
| Mary | Sheming | 1845 | Martlesham | 89 |
| Israel | Shipley | 1844 | Gisleham | 92 |
| Leonard | Sitch | 1918 | Stowmarket | 121 |
| John | Smith | 1812 | Cookley | 47 |
| Elizabeth | Smith | 1812 | Cookley | 47 |
| Fred | Southgate | 1924 | Ardleigh (Essex) | 120 |
| Joseph | Speller | 1831 | Bury St. Edmunds | 14 |
| James | Steggles | 1783 | Barrow | 45 |
| Henry | Steward | 1766 | Bury St. Edmunds | 42 |
| Frederick | Storey | 1920 | Ipswich | 120 |
| *Mary* | *Taylor* | *1731* | *Norfolk* | *15* |
| Louis | Thain | 1913 | Lowestoft | 121 |
| Jeremiah | Theobald (alias Hasel) | 1783 | Eriswell | 43 |
| Edmund | Thrower | 1812 | Cratfield | 85 |

| Name | | Date | Place | Page |
|---|---|---|---|---|
| John | Took | 1812 | Melton | 37 |
| William | Twitchett | 1832 | Stradishall | 83 |
| John | Vernon (alias Long Jack) | 1736 | London | 35 |
| Jonathan | Vincent | 1769 | Laxfield | 122 |
| John | Wade | 1822 | Hadleigh | 71 |
| John | Watling | 1753 | Carleton | 123 |
| John | Webb | 1819 | Exning | 13 |
| ____ | Weems | 1819 | Cambridge | 31 |
| Samuel | Wheeler | 1806 | Stradishall | 58 |
| George | Whistlecraft | 1929 | Botesdale | 121 |
| John | Wilkinson | 1785 | Felixstowe | 46 |
| Elizabeth | Wilkinson | 1785 | Felixstowe | 46 |
| John | Woodburne | 1721 | Bury St. Edmunds | 15 |
| John | Woods | 1753 | Woodbridge | 123 |
| Elizabeth | Woolterton | 1815 | North Cove | 64 |
| William | York | 1748 | Eyke | 12 |
| Alfred | Youngman | 1920 | Wickham Skeith | 121 |

Chained and manacled in the condemned cell

# Governors & Chaplains of the County Gaols

(Taken from Kelly's , White's and other Directories)

## BURY

| GAOL | Governor | Chaplain |
|------|----------|----------|
| 1830 | John Orridge | Thomas West |
| 1839 | John Orridge | |
| 1844 | John Orridge | |
| 1855 | Patrick McIntyre | Edward C. Wells |
| 1858 | Patrick McIntyre | Edward C. Wells |
| 1869 | Patrick McIntyre | Edward C. Wells |
| 1873 | Patrick McIntyre | J.W. Mills |
| 1874 | Maj. Montague Procter | Elijah H. Littlewood |
| 1875 | Capt. A.W. Twyford | Elijah H. Littlewood |

**IN 1878, BURY GAOL WAS CLOSED AND THE PRISONERS HOUSED AT IPSWICH GAOL. IPSWICH GAOL CLOSED IN 1931**

## IPSWICH

| GAOL | Governor | Chaplain |
|------|----------|----------|
| 1830 | Samuel Johnson | |
| 1839 | Robert Fletcher | |
| 1844 | E.A. Johnson | J.R. Tunney |
| 1855 | Mr. John | John Edge Daniel |
| 1858 | William J.R. Tunmer | |
| 1864 | John Alloway | John Edge Daniel |
| 1869 | John Alloway | John Edge Daniel |
| 1873 | Capt. G.A. Crickitt | Henry R. Smythies |
| 1874 | Capt. G.A. Crickitt | Henry R. Smythies |
| 1879 | George Hulme | Granville V. Vickers-Smith |
| 1885 | George Hulme | Granville V. Vickers-Smith |
| 1888 | George Hulme | Granville V. Vickers-Smith |
| 1890 | Mr. Ridge | Granville V. Vickers-Smith |
| 1892 | Maj. D. Matheson | Michael J. Sisson |
| 1896 | James Reader Groves (Chief Warder) | John Powell |
| 1900 | Mr. S. Gorsuch | John Powell |

Execution of Wm. Abigail, 19 years old,
May 22nd, 1882.

It was only on April 25th that Abigail shot
Jane Plunket dead in her bed. Within a
month he was captured, tried before the magis-
trates, committed for trial at the Assizes, condemned and hung. He made a confession of
his guilt, and seemed very penitent.

The fascination with executions continued long after public hangings ended. This announcement was published in the Hunstanton Telephone & West Norfolk Chronicle in May 1882.

# DEATH RECORDED

An EXCEL file of all those receiving death sentences from
Suffolk Assize Courts 1732 - 1900 and outcomes where known

Most information is from contemporary local newspapers.
Occasional information gleaned from court listings etc.

References to local newspapers:

**IJ**    Ipswich Journal
**SC**   Suffolk Chronicle
**BP**   Bury & Norwich Post
**BFP**  Bury Free Press
**NG**  Norwich Gazette
**IG**   Ipswich Gazette
**SM**  Suffolk Mercury
**NM**  Norwich Mercury
**NC**  Norfolk Chronicle

Those highlighted in grey are cases covered in detail
in this book.   Those in bold type resulted in hangings.

This has not been indexed.   Those wishing to purchase a copy of
the computer file on CD or floppy disk should refer to the **'Death
Recorded'** page on my website **www.pipwright.com.**

| Date of trial report | Year | Christian name | Surname | Age | Place offence committed | Crime | Outcome |
|---|---|---|---|---|---|---|---|
| Apr 1st NG | 1732 | Jeremiah | F(r)iske | | | Housebreaking | **Executed at Ipswich on April 15th** Details: Norwich Gazette April 22nd |
| Apr 1st NG | 1732 | John | Potter | | | Housebreaking | Outcome unknown |
| Apr 1st NG | 1732 | Andrews | Irons | | | Felony & Burglary | Outcome unknown |
| Apr 1st NG | 1732 | Edward | Wells | | | Horse Stealing | Outcome unknown |
| Apr 1st NG | 1732 | Philip | Ellis | | | Horse Stealing | **Executed at Ipswich on April 15th** Details: Norwich Gazette April 22nd |
| Mar 17th IG | 1733 | Samuel | Partridge | 22 | | Highway robbery | **Executed at Ipswich on March 31st** |
| Mar 17th IG | 1733 | Samuel | Kingsbury | | | Breaking into a shop & stealing watches | Respited, and presumed reprieved |
| Aug 4th IG | 1733 | | Scot (may be his surname or he may have come from Scotland) | | | Horse stealing | Reprieved |
| Mar 30th IG | 1734 | John | Norton | | | Poisoning his wife | **Unknown, presumed hanged** |
| Mar 30th IG | 1734 | George | Lane | | | Horse stealing | **Unknown, presumed hanged** |
| Aug 10th IG | 1734 | Unnamed person | | | | | Minimal information - 2 were capitally convicted, both of whom were reprieved and transported |
| Aug 10th IG | 1734 | Unnamed person | | | | | |
| Mar 22nd IG | 1735 | Robert | Bird | 30 | Ipswich | Stealing a mare | **Executed at Ipswich on April 12th.** Details: IG April 19th |
| Mar 22nd IG | 1735 | Samuel | Smith | | | Horse stealing | Reprieved |
| Mar 22nd IG | 1735 | Robert | Lambert | 26 | Letheringham | Housebreaking | **Hanged at Wilton Hill, Melton on April 9th** |
| Mar 22nd IG | 1735 | Ann | Pitts | | | Robbing her master | Reprieved |

| Date of trial report | Year | Christian name | Surname | Age | Place offence committed | Crime | Outcome |
|---|---|---|---|---|---|---|---|
| Mar 22nd IG | 1735 | Richard | Prince | | | Arson & robbery of his master | Reprieved |
| Aug 2nd IG | 1735 | John | Willson, alias 'Old York' | | Semer | Murder of a dragoon - he was a smuggler trying to avoid arrest | Brought from London for trial. **Hanged at Hadleigh on August 8th.** Details: IG April 26th, August 9th. |
| Aug 2nd IG | 1735 | John | Biggs | | Semer | Murder of a dragoon - he was a smuggler trying to avoid arrest | Brought from London for trial. **Hanged at Hadleigh on August 8th.** Details: IG April 26th, August 9th. |
| Aug 2nd IG | 1735 | Samuel | Bitman | | | Horse stealing | Reprieved and 'cast for transportation.' |
| Aug 2nd IG | 1735 | (a girl, | | 13 | | Arson | Reprieved and 'cast for transportation.' |
| Aug 2nd IG | 1735 | | Colman | | | Stealing a watch | Reprieved and 'cast for transportation.' |
| Mar 27th IG | 1736 | John | Bearth or Britt | | Capel near Butley | Murder of his wife | **Executed on April 7th** Details: IG February 7th & April 10th |
| Mar 27th IG | 1736 | George | Chandler | | | Horse stealing | **Executed on April 10th** |
| Mar 27th IG | 1736 | (a boy, unnamed) | | | | Stealing a pair of breeches with money in them, from | Probably reprieved |
| Sept 4th IG | 1736 | Phillip | Ward alias Ratts | | | Horse Stealing (or housebreaking) | **Hanged at Ipswich on September 18th** Details: Norwich Mercury September 25th |
| Sept 4th IG | 1736 | Samuel | Sayer | | | Horse stealing | Reprieved and sent for transportation for 14 years - reported NM September 25th |
| Sept 4th IG | 1736 | William | Whitman | | | Horse stealing | **Hanged at Ipswich on September 18th** Details: Norwich Mercury September 25th |
| Sept 4th IG | 1736 | John | Howard | | | Housebreaking (or shoplifting) | **Hanged at Ipswich on September 18th** Details: Norwich Mercury September 25th |

| Date of trial report | Year | Christian name | Surname | Age | Place offence committed | Crime | Outcome |
|---|---|---|---|---|---|---|---|
| Sept 4th IG | 1736 | Thomas | Adcock | | | Burglary | Reprieved and sent for transportation for 14 years - reported NM September 25th |
| Sept 4th IG | 1736 | James | Mallet | | | Horse stealing | Reprieved and sent for transportation for 14 years - reported NM September 25th |
| Mar 21st SM | 1737 | John | Crisp | | | Highway Robbery | Reprieved |
| Mar 21st SM | 1737 | **John** | **Wallidge (or Wallace)** | | | Housebreaking | **Executed at Bury on March 30th** Details: SM April 4th |
| Mar 21st SM | 1737 | **John** | **Kitchen** | | | Housebreaking | **Executed at Ipswich on April 2nd** |
| Mar 21st SM | 1737 | **Berrel** | **Kitchen** | | | Housebreaking | **Executed at Ipswich on April 2nd** |
| Mar 21st SM | 1737 | **John** | **Bicker** | | | Shoplifting | **Executed at Bury on March 30th** Details: SM April 4th |
| Mar 21st SM | 1737 | John | Brewster | | | Stealing 2 mares | Reprieved |
| SUMMER ASSIZE | **1737** | **NO SURVIVING REPORTS** | | | | | |
| LENT ASSIZE | **1738** | **NO SURVIVING REPORTS** | | | | | |
| SUMMER ASSIZE | **1738** | **NO SURVIVING REPORTS** | | | | | |
| | 1738 | William | Blois | | | | Reprieved and sent for transportation for 14 years (reported IJ March 31st 1739) |
| Apr 7th IJ | 1739 | **Richard** | **Gathercole** | | Icklingham | Burglary | No further details - **presumed hanged** |
| Apr 7th IJ | 1739 | **Isaac** | **Jakes** | | Sudbury | Burglary | No further details - **presumed hanged** |

| Date of trial report | Year | Christian name | Surname | Age | Place offence committed | Crime | Outcome |
|---|---|---|---|---|---|---|---|
| Aug 18th IJ | 1739 | Christopher | Last | | | | Probably received sentence of death but reprieved and transported |
| Aug 18th IJ | 1739 | Stafford | Brinslow | | | | Probably received sentence of death but reprieved and transported |
| Mar 29th IJ | 1740 | Charles | Drew | | Melford | Murder of his father | **Hanged on April 9th.** Details: IJ March 29th & April 12th. Was spared being hung in chains |
| Mar 29th IJ | 1740 | James | Curry | | | Highway robbery | Reprieved; later pardoned and discharged (IJ August 9th 1740) |
| Aug 9th IJ | 1740 | John | Ablet | | | Horse stealing | Reprieved - but as is shown below, he was tried & hanged for another offence at the next Assize. |
| Mar 28th IJ | 1741 | John | Knights | | | Housebreaking | **Sent for execution at Bury April 1st** (not reported) |
| Mar 28th IJ | 1741 | John | Garnham | | | Housebreaking | **Sent for execution at Ipswich on April 4th** (not reported) |
| Mar 28th IJ | 1741 | James | Garnham | | | Housebreaking | **Sent for execution at Ipswich on April 4th** (not reported) |
| Mar 28th IJ | 1741 | John | Ablet | | Bredfield | Housebreaking | **Sent for execution at Ipswich on April 4th** (not reported) |
| Mar 28th IJ | 1741 | Robert | Cullum | | | Horse stealing | Reprieved and sent for transportation for 14 years (reported IJ July 25th) |
| Mar 28th IJ | 1741 | William | Bell | | | Horse stealing | **Sent for execution at Bury April 1st** (not reported) |
| Mar 28th IJ | 1741 | George | Warren | | Glemsford | Housebreaking | Reprieved and sent for transportation for 14 years (reported IJ July 25th) |
| July 25th IJ | 1741 | Richard | Baker | | | Felony & burglary | **Executed at Bury on July 29th** (reported IJ August 8th) |
| July 25th IJ | 1741 | Henry | Crack | | | Felony & burglary | **Executed at Ipswich on August 1st** (reported IJ August 8th) |

| Date of trial report | Year | Christian name | Surname | Age | Place offence committed | Crime | Outcome |
|---|---|---|---|---|---|---|---|
| Mar 27th IJ | 1742 | Thomas | Gibbs | | | Burglary | Reprieved (IJ April 3rd) Later transported for 14 years (IJ August 14th) |
| Mar 27th IJ | 1742 | Thomas | Cheany | | | Burglary | **Sent for execution at Ipswich on April 10th** (not reported) |
| Mar 27th IJ | 1742 | William | Townshend | | | Horse stealing | **Sent for execution at Bury April 7th** (reported IJ April 10th) |
| Mar 27th IJ | 1742 | John | Parker | | | Horse stealing | Reprieved but held for another offence - see below |
| Mar 27th IJ | 1742 | John | Flower | | | Highway robbery | **Sent for execution at Bury April 7th** (reported IJ April 10th) |
| Mar 27th IJ | 1742 | Mary | Bush | | | Stealing clothing | Reprieved (IJ April 3rd) Later transported for 14 years (IJ August 14th) |
| Mar 27th IJ | 1742 | Robert | Reeve | | | Returning from transportation, horse stealing & highway robbery | **Sent for execution at Bury April 7th** (reported IJ April 10th) |
| Mar 27th IJ | 1742 | Joseph | Barham | | | Sheep stealing | Reprieved and sent for 14 years transportation (reported IJ March 26th 1743) |
| Aug 14th IJ | 1742 | Robert | Chinery | | | Sheep stealing | Reprieved and sent for 14 years transportation (reported IJ March 26th 1743) |
| Aug 14th IJ | 1742 | Zachary | Thompson | | | Sheep stealing | Reprieved and sent for 14 years transportation (reported IJ March 26th 1743) |
| Aug 14th IJ | 1742 | John | Parker | | | Forgery | Reprieved |

| Date of trial report | Year | Christian name | Surname | Age | Place offence committed | Crime | Outcome |
|---|---|---|---|---|---|---|---|
| Aug 14th IJ | 1742 | George | Crisp alias John Baker | | | Horse stealing - removed by Habeas Corpus from Chelmsford gaol | Reprieved and sent for 14 years transportation (reported IJ March 26th 1743) |
| Mar 26th IJ | 1743 | **William** | **Dodward** | | Bury St. Edmunds | Breaking open a drawer & stealing £11 | **Sentence of death; probably hanged but** not reported |
| Mar 26th IJ | 1743 | Robert | Armstrong | | | Horse stealing | Reprieved and sent for 14 years transportation (reported IJ August 6th) |
| Aug 6th IJ | 1743 | **James** | **Cheese** | | | Felony | **Sentence of death; probably hanged but** not reported |
| Aug 6th IJ | 1743 | William | Hunt | | | Felony | Reprieved and sent for 14 years transportation (reported March 31st 1744) |
| Mar 31st IJ | 1744 | Joseph | Rugles alias Everret | | | Housebreaking | No mention of reprieve, but as he was still in gaol on July 28th, it is presumed he did not hang. |
| Mar 31st IJ | 1744 | Joseph | Dansie | | | Housebreaking | Reprieved and sent for transportation for 14 years (reported IJ July 28th) |
| Mar 31st IJ | 1744 | John | Clarke | | | Housebreaking | Reprieved and sent for transportation for 14 years (reported IJ July 28th) |
| Mar 31st IJ | 1744 | William | Emms | | | Horse stealing | Reprieved and sent for transportation for 14 years (reported IJ July 28th) |
| July 28th IJ | 1744 | Peter | Pearse (or Pearce) | | Nayland | Housebreaking | Reprieved and sent for transportation for 14 years (reported IJ March 30th 1745) |
| Mar 30th IJ | 1745 | John | Wyard | | | Sheep stealing | Reprieved a week later and sent for transportation for 14 years (reported IJ April 6th & August 10th) |

| Date of trial report | Year | Christian name | Surname | Age | Place offence committed | Crime | Outcome |
|---|---|---|---|---|---|---|---|
| Mar 30th IJ | 1745 | John | Fuller | | | Horse stealing | Reprieved a week later and sent for transportation for 14 years (reported IJ April 6th & August 10th) |
| Mar 30th IJ | 1745 | Sarah | Lock | | | Murder of her bastard child | Reprieved a week later and sent for transportation for 14 years (reported IJ April 6th & August 10th) |
| Mar 30th IJ | 1745 | Richard | Peacock | | | Felony | Reprieved a week later and sent for transportation for 14 years (reported IJ April 6th & August 10th) |
| Aug 10th IJ | 1745 | Thomas | Peake | | Westhall | Housebreaking | Reprieved and sent for transportation for 14 years (reported IJ March 22nd 1746) |
| Aug 10th IJ | 1745 | John | King | | Milden | Stealing a mare | Reprieved and sent for transportation for 14 years (reported IJ March 22nd 1746) |
| Aug 10th IJ | 1745 | William | Fuller | | Monks Eleigh | Burglary | Reprieved and sent for transportation for 14 years (reported IJ March 22nd 1746) |
| Aug 10th IJ | 1745 | Elizabeth | Macdonald | | | Picking pockets | Reprieved and sent for transportation for 14 years (reported IJ March 22nd 1746) |
| Mar 22nd IJ | 1746 | **William** | **Rook** | | | Housebreaking | **Probably hanged, but not reported** |
| Mar 22nd IJ | 1746 | **Daniel** | **Partridge** | | | Housebreaking | **Probably hanged, but not reported** |
| Apr 11th IJ | 1747 | John | Osborne | | | Robbery | Reprieved |
| SUMMER ASSIZE (Aug 12th) | **1747** | **NOT REPORTED** | | | | | |

| Date of trial report | Year | Christian name | Surname | Age | Place offence committed | Crime | Outcome |
|---|---|---|---|---|---|---|---|
| Mar 19th IJ | 1748 | **Stephen** | **Pettit** | | Ipswich | Murder - he stabbed a sergeant | **Executed at Ipswich on April 2nd** Reported IJ April 9th Details of murder: IJ March 5th |
| Aug 6th IJ | 1748 | William | York | | Eyke | Murder of another child - he was 10 | Sentence of death deferred twice; eventually reprieved and pardoned |
| Apr 1st IJ | 1749 | **John** | **Gaifer** | | Capel | Stealing 20 sheep | **Executed at Ipswich on April 8th** (reported IJ April 15th) |
| Aug 12th IJ | 1749 | Jonathan | Paul | | | Horse stealing | Reprieved and sent for transportation for 14 years (reported IJ March 31st 1750) |
| Aug 12th IJ | 1749 | Thomas | Johnson | | | Horse stealing | Reprieved and sent for transportation for 14 years (reported IJ March 31st 1750) |
| Mar 31st IJ | 1750 | **Thomas** | **Martin** | | | Highway robbery | **Sent for execution April 5th.** Presumed hanged but not reported. |
| Mar 31st IJ | 1750 | John | Johnson | | | Highway robbery | Reprieved |
| Aug 25th IJ | 1750 | **Toby** | **Gill** | | Blythburgh | Murder and rape | **Executed and hanged in chains at Blythburgh on September 14th** Details: IJ September 15th |
| Aug 25th IJ | 1750 | William | Cullum | | Trimley | Horse stealing | Reprieved and sent for transportation for 14 years (reported IJ March 30th 1751) |
| Aug 25th IJ | 1750 | John | Scott | | Trimley | Horse stealing | Reprieved and sent for transportation for 14 years (reported IJ March 30th 1751) |
| Mar 30th IJ | 1751 | **James** | **Dunn** | | Botesdale | Housebreaking, with threats of murder | **Executed (presumably at Ipswich) April 6th 1751** |
| Mar 30th IJ | 1751 | Digby | Brown-Smith | | | Sheep stealing | Reprieved and ordered for transportation |

| Date of trial report | Year | Christian name | Surname | Age | Place offence committed | Crime | Outcome |
|---|---|---|---|---|---|---|---|
| Mar 30th IJ | 1751 | William | Shearing | | | Horse stealing | Reprieved and ordered for transportation |
| Aug 3rd IJ | 1751 | Thomas | Brook | | Blakenham | Housebreaking in 1748 - brought by Habeas Corpus from Newgate. | **Executed at Ipswich on August 6th** Details: IJ August 10th |
| Aug 3rd IJ | 1751 | John | Cunningham | | Blakenham | Housebreaking in 1748 - brought by Habeas Corpus from Newgate. | **Executed at Ipswich on August 6th** Details: IJ August 10th |
| Aug 3rd IJ | 1751 | Francis | Mayhew | | Blakenham | Housebreaking in 1748 - brought by Habeas Corpus from Newgate. | **Executed at Ipswich on August 6th** Details: IJ August 10th |
| Aug 3rd IJ | 1751 | Robert | Clarke | | Botesdale | Housebreaking, linked to James Dunn case above | **Executed at Ipswich on August 6th** Details: IJ August 10th |
| Mar 28th IJ | 1752 | Thomas | Fidget (commonly known as White-eyes) | | Felixstowe | Murder - he was a notorious smuggler and was resisting arrest | Associated with the gang above in the Blakenham burglary and others. **Executed at Ipswich on April 9th.** Details: IJ April 11th |
| Mar 28th IJ | 1752 | John | Ward alias Newman | | | Horse stealing | Executed at Ipswich on April 9th. Details: IJ April 11th |
| Mar 28th IJ | 1752 | John | Osborne jun. | | | Breaking into a warehouse, stealing 60 shillings | Reprieved |
| Aug 1st IJ | 1752 | Thomas | Otley | | Sudbury | Murder of his wife | **Taken from Bury Gaol & executed on July 27th,** then *'hung in chains on Black Close Hill, near the road to Newmarket.'* Details: IJ August 1st |
| April 7th IJ | 1753 | Samuel | Hill | | | Sheep stealing | Reprieved and ordered for 14 years transportation |

| Date of trial report | Year | Christian name | Surname | Age | Place offence committed | Crime | Outcome |
|---|---|---|---|---|---|---|---|
| April 7th IJ | 1753 | Thomas | Hill | | | Sheep stealing | Reprieved and ordered for 14 years transportation |
| April 7th IJ | 1753 | John | Kemp | | | Horse stealing | Reprieved and ordered for 14 years transportation |
| Aug 18th IJ | 1753 | **John** | **Watling** | | Carleton | Housebreaking | **Executed at Ipswich on September 1st** |
| Aug 18th IJ | 1753 | **John** | **Woods (real name later discovered to be Peter Lilliston)** | | Woodbridge | Highway robbery | **Executed at Ipswich on September 1st** |
| Aug 18th IJ | 1753 | William | Mann | | | Stealing 34 sheep | Reprieved and sent for transportation for 14 years (reported IJ April 6th 1754) |
| Aug 18th IJ | 1753 | John | Kent | | Kessingland | Housebreaking | Reprieved and sent for transportation for 14 years (reported IJ April 6th 1754) |
| April 6th IJ | 1754 | James | Beckett | | Walpole | Horse stealing | Sentence of death, later reprieved to transportation for 14 years (reported IJ August 17th 1854) |
| April 6th IJ | 1754 | **William** | **Webber** | | Polstead | Housebreaking | **Probably hanged**, but not reported in IJ or NM |
| April 6th IJ | 1754 | John | English | | Barking | Rape | Reprieved and sent for transportation for 14 years (reported IJ August 17th 1754) |
| April 6th IJ | 1754 | Robert | Burt | | | Horse stealing | Reprieved and sent for transportation for 14 years (reported IJ August 17th 1754) |
| Aug 17th IJ | 1754 | **William** | **Scott alias Taylor** | | Ipswich | Forgery | **Executed at Ipswich on September 4th** |

| Date of trial report | Year | Christian name | Surname | Age | Place offence committed | Crime | Outcome |
|---|---|---|---|---|---|---|---|
| Aug 17th IJ | 1754 | **Thomas** | **Land** | | Bramford | Highway robbery | **Executed at Ipswich on September 4th** Details: IJ July 13th |
| Apr 5th IJ | 1755 | John | Moyes alias Pearson | | Covehithe | Housebreaking | Reprieved and sent for transportation for 14 years (reported IJ July 26th 1755) |
| Apr 5th IJ | 1755 | John | Brand | | Spexhall | Stealing a mare | Reprieved and sent for transportation for 14 years (reported IJ July 26th 1755) |
| Mar 27th/Apr 3rd IJ | 1756 | **Thomas** | **Herring** | | Stowmarket | Highway robbery and horse theft | **Executed on April 10th.** Mr. Bacon, his victim paid 10 guineas reward for his capture. Advert for trial booklet IJ April 17th |
| Sept 3rd IJ | 1757 | Thomas | Callow | | | Housebreaking | No further detail other than he received a capital sentence |
| Apr 1st IJ | 1758 | **John** | **Slayter** | | Trimley | Highway robbery | Described as a foot soldier, **probably hanged as intended on April 8th** |
| Apr 1st IJ | 1758 | Michael | Wright | | Bury St. Edmunds | Extortion | Reprieved. Sent for 14 years transportation (reported IJ August 12th) |
| Apr 1st IJ | 1758 | William | Fuller | | | Horse stealing | Reprieved. Sent for 14 years transportation (reported IJ August 12th) |
| Aug 12th IJ | 1758 | Richard | Ashwell | | Ufford | Highway robbery | Reprieved (reported IJ August 26th) |
| Mar 31st IJ | 1759 | Mary | Walker | | Hartest | Stealing meat | Reprieved |
| Mar 31st IJ | 1759 | | Hall | | Shotley | Robbery | Described as a soldier, **set for execution on April 7th** - probably hanged |

| Date of trial report | Year | Christian name | Surname | Age | Place offence committed | Crime | Outcome |
|---|---|---|---|---|---|---|---|
| Mar 31st IJ | 1759 | | **Mortenshaw** | | Shotley | Robbery | Described as a soldier, **set for execution on April 7th** - probably hanged |
| Aug 18th IJ | 1759 | Robert | Woods | | Blyford | Stealing a mare | Reprieved & sent for transportation for 14 years (reported IJ March 22nd 1760) |
| Mar 22nd IJ | 1760 | Thomas | Buck | | Little Glemham | | Sentence of death, reprieved April 29th, sent for 14 years transportation (reported IJ August 2nd 1760) |
| Mar 22nd IJ | 1760 | Benjamin | Buck | | Little Glemham | | Sentence of death, reprieved April 29th, sent for 14 years transportation (reported IJ August 2nd 1760) |
| Mar 22nd IJ | 1760 | **Thomas** | **Kersey** | | Great Thornham | | **Ordered for execution April 12th.** Application for reprieve *proved ineffectual.* Reported hanged IJ April 19th |
| Mar 21st IJ | 1761 | **Edward** | **Johnson** | | | Murder of his apprentice - he was a chimney sweeper | **Sentenced to hang in Chains on March 23rd (IJ) but reported** hanged on March 20th in NM March 21st |
| Aug 14th IJ | 1762 | Mones | Dorling | | | Theft & forgery | Reprieved. Sent for transportation for life (reported IJ March 26th 1763) |
| Mar 26th IJ | 1763 | **Margery** | **Beddingfield** | | Sternfield | Murder of husband (petty treason) | Strangled and burnt at the stake at Ipswich on April 8th. Details: IJ April 2nd & 9th |
| Mar 26th IJ | 1763 | **Richard** | **Ring(e)** | | Sternfield | Murder | Hanged at Ipswich on April 8th. Details: IJ April 2nd & 9th |
| Mar 26th IJ | 1763 | John | Culling | | | Sodomy of a boy aged 11 | Execution deferred as he was suffering from smallpox. Details: IJ April 2nd & 23rd. His Majesty's free pardon - IJ August 6th. |

| Date of trial report | Year | Christian name | Surname | Age | Place offence committed | Crime | Outcome |
|---|---|---|---|---|---|---|---|
| Mar 24th IJ | 1764 | Matthew | Hindes | | | Stealing a cow | Reprieved and sent for transportation for 14 years (IJ August 18th 1764) |
| Apr 6th | 1765 | William | Blake | | Beccles | Horse stealing | Reprieved and sent for transportation for 14 years (IJ August 3rd 1765) |
| Apr 6th | 1765 | Robert | Clodd (or Thobald) | | | Horse stealing | Reprieved and sent for transportation for 14 years (IJ August 3rd 1765) |
| Apr 6th | 1765 | Robert | Meek | | | Sheep stealing | Reprieved and sent for transportation for 14 years (IJ August 3rd 1765) |
| Mar 22nd IJ | 1766 | Elizabeth | Burroughs | | Bury St. Edmunds | Murder | **Executed at Bury on April 4th.** Details: IJ March 22nd & April 5th |
| Mar 22nd IJ | 1766 | John | Brock (or Brook) | | Thorndon | Housebreaking - stole £100 | **Set to hang on April 10th at Ipswich. No newspaper record of this being carried out, though other evidence shows it was.** |
| Mar 22nd IJ | 1766 | John | Francis | | Thorndon | Housebreaking - stole £100 | **Set to hang on April 10th at Ipswich. No newspaper record of this being carried out, though other evidence shows it was.** |
| Mar 22nd IJ | 1766 | Joseph | Browning | | Cretingham | Stealing a mare | Reprieved - sent for transportation for 14 years (NM August 2nd) |
| Aug 2nd IJ | 1766 | George | Dorman alias Sims | | Methwold, Nfk. | Horse stealing | Reprieved - listed for transportation (IJ March 28th 1767) |
| Aug 2nd IJ | 1766 | John | Layt alias Johnson | | Methwold, Nfk. | Horse stealing | Reprieved - listed for transportation (IJ March 28th 1767) |
| Aug 2nd IJ | 1766 | John | Smith | | Debenham | Stealing money | Reprieved - listed for transportation (IJ March 28th 1767) |
| Mar 28th IJ | 1767 | William | Studd | | | Burglary | Reprieved - listed for transportation for 14 years (IJ August 15th 1767) |
| Mar 28th IJ | 1767 | Charles | Cable | | | Horse stealing | Reprieved - listed for transportation for 14 years (IJ August 15th 1767) |

| Date of trial report | Year | Christian name | Surname | Age | Place offence committed | Crime | Outcome |
|---|---|---|---|---|---|---|---|
| Mar 28th IJ | 1767 | Elizabeth | Stannard | | | Robbery | Reprieved - listed for transportation for 14 years (IJ August 15th 1767) |
| Mar 28th IJ | 1767 | Elizabeth | Brock | | | Robbery | Reprieved - listed for transportation for 14 years (IJ August 15th 1767) |
| July 30th IJ | 1768 | Martha | Green | | | Robbing her mistress | Executed at Ipswich on August 13th |
| July 30th IJ | 1768 | Thomas | Thorpe | | | Stealing a watch | Reprieved |
| Mar 25th IJ | 1769 | John | Hainsworth | | Lowestoft | Burglary | Set to hang at Ipswich on the 22nd April, but no report it was ever carried out. |
| Mar 25th IJ | 1769 | William | Witson | | Lowestoft | Burglary | Reprieve reported April 8th, then he was listed to hang on the 22nd April, but no report that it was ever carried out. |
| Mar 25th IJ | 1769 | Isaac | Skinner | 22 | Bures | Stealing an elm plank and returning from transportation | Executed at Bury on April 12th  Detail of execution: NM April 15th |
| Mar 25th IJ | 1769 | Ben | Deer | | | Horse stealing | Reprieved |
| July 22nd IJ | 1769 | Jonathan | Vincent | | Laxfield | Murder of his bastard child | Executed at Ipswich on July 20th. Details: IJ June 3rd & July 22nd |
| July 22nd IJ | 1769 | William | Fleet | | Gorleston | Robbery | Reprieved and sent for transportation (NM July 22nd) He had been reprieved from a death sentence in Norfolk in 1765 along with his mother and sister. |
| Mar 31st IJ | 1770 | William | Chandley | | | Horse stealing | Reprieved |
| Mar 31st IJ | 1770 | James | Green | | | Horse stealing | Reprieved |
| Mar 31st IJ | 1770 | Robert | Tye | | | Horse stealing | Reprieved |
| Aug 18th IJ | 1770 | Henry | Whitton | | | Horse stealing | Reprieved and listed for transportation (IJ August 25th) |
| Aug 18th IJ | 1770 | John | Hurren | | | Horse stealing | Reprieved and listed for transportation (IJ August 25th) |

| Date of trial report | Year | Christian name | Surname | Age | Place offence committed | Crime | Outcome |
|---|---|---|---|---|---|---|---|
| Mar 30th IJ | 1771 | Edmund | Hunt | | | Stealing a cow | Reprieved |
| Mar 30th IJ | 1771 | John | Beaumont | | | Burglary | Executed at Ipswich on April 13th. Reported IJ April 20th |
| Mar 30th IJ | 1771 | Ann | Catchpole | | | Arson | Executed at Ipswich on April 13th. Reported IJ April 20th |
| Aug 3rd IJ | 1771 | Susan | Dunwich | | | Murder of her bastard child | **Executed at Ipswich on July 31st** |
| Aug 10thNM | 1771 | Samuel | Place | | | Burglary & robbery | Reprieved |
| Aug 3rd IJ | 1771 | Ann | Place | | | Burglary & robbery | Reprieved |
| Aug 22nd IJ | 1772 | David | Pigney | | | Forgery | **Executed at Ipswich on September 12th** |
| Mar 20th IJ | 1773 | John | Mayhew | | | Horse stealing | Reprieved |
| Mar 20th IJ | 1773 | Henry | Flatt | | | Horse stealing | Reprieved |
| Mar 20th IJ | 1773 | William | Bolton (or Maddox) | | Thwaite (Buck's Head) | Burglary | Reprieved and ordered for transportation, but escaped. Details & advert IJ April 10th. Recaptured 4 years later - see details below for 1777 |
| Mar 20th IJ | 1773 | John | Blake | | Thwaite (Buck's Head) | Burglary | Reprieved |
| Mar 27th IJ | 1773 | Stephen | Bootman | | | Burglary | Reprieved |
| Mar 26th IJ | 1774 | Humphrey | Scott | | | Housebreaking | **Executed at Bury on April 20th** after a week's respite. |
| Mar 26th IJ | 1774 | Fletcher | Martin | | removed from Chelmsford gaol | Horse stealing | Reprieved (IJ April 2nd) |
| Mar 26th IJ | 1774 | Christopher | How | | | Sheep stealing | Reprieved (IJ April 2nd) |
| Mar 26th IJ | 1774 | John | Hardy | | | Sheep stealing | Reprieved (IJ April 2nd) |
| Mar 26th IJ | 1774 | William | Horn | | | Sheep stealing | Reprieved (IJ April 2nd) |
| Aug 8th IJ | 1774 | Edward | Abbot | | | Stealing 40 guineas | reprieved |
| Apr 1st IJ | 1775 | Robert | Cresswell | | | Housebreaking | reprieved |

| Date of trial report | Year | Christian name | Surname | Age | Place offence committed | Crime | Outcome |
|---|---|---|---|---|---|---|---|
| Apr 1st IJ | 1775 | William | Sampson | | | Housebreaking | reprieved |
| Apr 1st IJ | 1775 | James | Caudell | | | Horse stealing | reprieved |
| *Apr 1st IJ* | *1775* | *George* | *Smith* | | *Debenham* | *Murder* | *Left to next Assize as principal witness was unable to attend* |
| Aug 19th IJ | 1775 | John | Tillot | | Little Cornard | Stealing a gelding | reprieved |
| Aug 19th IJ | 1775 | John | Potter | | Ipswich | Robbery | reprieved |
| Aug 19th IJ | 1775 | Richard | Simpson | | Ipswich | Robbery | reprieved |
| Aug 19th IJ | 1775 | **George** | **Smith** | | Debenham | Murder - poisoned his wife | Sentenced to death;  **executed at Rushmere on August 19th** |
| Aug 10th IJ | 1776 | John | Alderton | | Needham Market | Robbery | reprieved |
| Aug 10th IJ | 1776 | George | Clarke | | Sutton | Stealing a gelding | reprieved |
| Mar 22nd IJ | 1777 | William | Maddox alias Bo(u)lton | | Thwaite | Rearrested, having escaped from a condemned sentence for burglary 4 years earlier and spent time in America | Sentenced to death; (details IJ March 15th & 22nd), respited (IJ March 29th), pardoned and discharged by proclamation (IJ July 26th 1777)     See details above for 1773 |
| Mar 22nd IJ | 1777 | **Edmund** | **Eastoe** | | | Murder of a soldier as he was smuggling | Sentenced to death and **hanged at Rushmere on March 22nd.**  Details of execution IJ March 29th |
| Mar 28th IJ | 1778 | Isaac | Whayman | | Ipswich | Forgery | Sentence of death, twice ordered for execution, but probably reprieved (IJ August 15th reports he remains in prison on respite during His Majesty's pleasure) |
| Mar 28th IJ | 1778 | James | Kilborne | | Buxhall | Burglary | Reprieved (IJ April 18th reports him cutting his hand most terribly to prevent serving in the army or on the Thames) |

| Date of trial report | Year | Christian name | Surname | Age | Place offence committed | Crime | Outcome |
|---|---|---|---|---|---|---|---|
| Aug 15th IJ | 1778 | Florence Robert | Sullivan | | | Stealing a mare | Reprieved |
| Aug 15th IJ | 1778 | Thomas | King | | Bury | Gaol breaking whilst under sentence of transportation | Reprieved |
| Mar 20th IJ | 1779 | **William** | **Lay** | | Ipswich | Burglary | Sentence of death. Deferred 7 days by the Sheriff to accompany Hoy's respite. **Hanged - Rushmere April 10th,** after attempting to escape. Details: IJ March 20th, April 17th. |
| Mar 20th IJ | 1779 | **Robert** | **Hoy** | | Brantham | Burglary | Sentence of death, respited 7 days on request of the Ordinary, Rev. Rich. Brome. **Hanged - Rushmere April 10th,** after attempting to escape. Details: IJ March 20th, April 17th. |
| Mar 20th IJ | 1779 | William | Sorril | | | Burglary | Sentence of death, reprieved |
| Mar 20th IJ | 1779 | Richard | Chimmins | | | Burglary | Sentence of death, reprieved |
| Mar 20th IJ | 1779 | Richard | Arstin | | | Sheep stealing | Sentence of death, reprieved |
| July 31st IJ | 1779 | Robert | Capon | | | Horse stealing | Sentence of death, reprieved |
| Mar 25th IJ | 1780 | **Jonathan** | **Sawyer alias Lock** | 18 | Cretingham & Brundish | Housebreaking | **Hanged - Rushmere April 8th** |
| Mar 25th IJ | 1780 | John | Patrick | | Ipswich | Burglary | reprieved - enlisted as a soldier |
| Mar 25th IJ | 1780 | Samuel | Clarke | | Ipswich | Stealing cloth | reprieved - joined East India Company |
| Mar 25th IJ | 1780 | George | Cranmer | | Ipswich | Stealing cloth | reprieved - joined East India Company |
| Aug 11th IJ | 1781 | Richard | Cuthbert | | | Robbery | reprieved |
| Aug 11th IJ | 1781 | Robert | Goodwin | | Debenham | Stealing a mare | reprieved |
| Aug 11th IJ | 1781 | Samuel | Smith | | Gedding | Sheep stealing | reprieved |

| Date of trial report | Year | Christian name | Surname | Age | Place offence committed | Crime | Outcome |
|---|---|---|---|---|---|---|---|
| Mar 23rd IJ | 1782 | John | Baldwin | | Ipswich St. Matthew | Horse stealing | NC March 23rd says he was sent for execution, but NM says he was reprieved. Details of arrest: IJ February 2nd |
| Mar 23rd IJ | 1782 | Mary | Welden alias Jealous | | Bury | Robbery | NC March 23rd says he was sent for execution, but NM says he was reprieved. |
| Mar 23rd IJ | 1782 | Mary | Goodman | | | Felony | Reprieved according to both Norfolk papers. |
| July 27th IJ | 1782 | John | Sones | | Sibton | Horse stealing | respited - serving His Majesty in Africa or East Indies |
| Mar 22nd/29th IJ | 1783 | John | Horn | | Higham | Sheep stealing | respited - April 5th & later sent to Woolwich for transportation. IJ March 24th 1787 |
| Mar 22nd/29th IJ | 1783 | **James** | **Steggles** | | **Barrow** | **Shooting at Mr. Macro** | **Hanged - Bury St. Edmunds April 2nd** |
| Mar 22nd/29th IJ | 1783 | Edward | Prime | | Chediston | Burglary | reprieved |
| Mar 22nd/29th IJ | 1783 | Robert | Prime | | Chediston | Burglary | reprieved |
| Mar 22nd/29th IJ | 1783 | William | Town(e)s | | Higham | Sheep stealing | respited April 5th Sent to Woolwich for transportation IJ March 24th 1787 |
| Mar 22nd/29th IJ | 1783 | Thomas | Palmer | | | Highway robbery | reprieved - later sent to Woolwich for transportation IJ March 24th 1787 |
| Mar 22nd/29th IJ | 1783 | *Benjamin* | *Wiseman* | | *Freckenham* | *Burglary* | *not capitally convicted as his confession helped convict May & Theobald (below) 2 yrs. Gaol* |
| Mar 22nd/29th IJ | 1783 | **Samuel** | **Roberts** | | Melford/Sudbury | Highway robbery | **Hanged - Bury St. Edmunds April 2nd** |

| Date of trial report | Year | Christian name | Surname | Age | Place offence committed | Crime | Outcome |
|---|---|---|---|---|---|---|---|
| Mar 22nd/29th IJ | 1783 | John | Roberts | | Melford/Sudbury | Highway robbery | reprieved |
| Mar 22nd/29th IJ | 1783 | Samuel | Clarke | | Tannington | Sheep stealing | reprieved & later sent to Woolwich for transportation  IJ March 24th 1787 |
| Mar 22nd/29th IJ | 1783 | **Samuel** | **Oxer** | | Sudbury | Burglary | **Hanged - Bury St. Edmunds April 2nd after attempting to escape** |
| Mar 22nd/29th IJ | 1783 | John | Payne | | Dalham | Sheep stealing | reprieved |
| Mar 22nd/29th IJ | 1783 | Daniel | Outlaw | | Dalham | Sheep stealing | reprieved |
| Mar 22nd/29th IJ | 1783 | William | Kilburn Sen. | | Hitcham | Stealing butter & cheese | reprieved |
| Mar 26th BP | 1783 | **James** | **May alias Folkes** | | Eriswell | Murder | **Hanged - Bury St. Edmunds, March 23rd, then hung in chains** Details BP October 31st 1782, March 26th 1783 |
| Mar 26th BP | 1783 | **Jeremiah** | **Theobald alias Hasell** | | Eriswell | Murder | **Hanged - Bury St. Edmunds, March 23rd, then hung in chains** Details BP October 31st 1782, March 26th 1783 |
| Aug 23rd IJ | 1783 | Elizabeth | Hart | | Stoke | Stealing a cloak | reprieved |
| Aug 23rd IJ | 1783 | Richard | Smith | | Lavenham | Robbery on a footpath | reprieved |
| Mar 27th IJ | 1784 | Thomas | Bird | 25 | Ashbocking | Highway robbery & Horse stealing | reprieved - escaped from Ipswich gaol with William Godbold - advert IJ May 29th 1784 |
| Mar 27th IJ | 1784 | *Nicholas* | *Goddard* | | *Combs* | *Burglary* | *Capitally convicted - left till next Assize as wrong date on warrant - see below* |
| Mar 27th IJ | 1784 | **William** | **Simpson** | | Hacheston | Burglary | **Hanged - Rushmere April 10th** |
| Mar 27th IJ | 1784 | **Joseph** | **Lambert** | | Hacheston | Burglary | **Hanged - Rushmere April 10th** |
| Mar 27th IJ | 1784 | John | Payne | | Barrow | Burglary | reprieved |

| Date of trial report | Year | Christian name | Surname | Age | Place offence committed | Crime | Outcome |
|---|---|---|---|---|---|---|---|
| Mar 27th IJ | 1784 | Robert | Crowfoot | | Ashbocking | Horse stealing | reprieved |
| Mar 27th IJ | 1784 | James | Riches | | Melton | Burglary | reprieved and transported to New South Wales for 14 years 1789. Died a week after arriving. |
| Mar 27th IJ | 1784 | Richard | Coates | | Pettaugh | Burglary | reprieved & later sent to Woolwich for transportation  IJ March 24th 1787 |
| Mar 27th IJ | 1784 | _____ | Wilding alias Warren | | Bury St. Edmunds | Stealing a watch | reprieved |
| Mar 27th IJ | 1784 | Elizabeth | Harvey | | Bungay | Burglary | reprieved |
| Aug 7th IJ | 1784 | Nicholas | Goddard | | Combs | Burglary | respited during His Majesty's pleasure |
| Aug 7th IJ | 1784 | John | Lenney | | Cratfield | Robbery | respited during His Majesty's Pleasure: sent to Woolwich for transportation  IJ March 24th 1787 |
| Aug 7th IJ | 1784 | Joseph | Hatley | | Melford | Robbery | respited |
| Aug 7th IJ | 1784 | **Joseph** | **Banks** | | Melford | Robbery | **Hanged - Bury August 18th** |
| Aug 7th IJ | 1784 | John | Murrils | | Newton | Stealing cows | reprieved |
| Mar 26th IJ | 1785 | Henry | Nunn alias Cooke | | Otley | Horse stealing | reprieved & later sent to Woolwich for transportation     IJ March 24th 1787 |
| Mar 26th IJ | 1785 | **Jonathan** | **Larter** | | Weybread | Robbery | **Hanged - Rushmere April 9th   Details: BP April 13th** |
| Mar 26th IJ | 1785 | **Abraham** | **Stow** | | Polstead | Robbery | **Hanged - Bury April 6th** |
| Mar 26th IJ | 1785 | **John** | **Wilkinson** | | Felixstowe | Murder of daughter | **Hanged - Rushmere March 28th details IJ April 2nd** |
| Mar 26th IJ | 1785 | **Elizabeth** | **Wilkinson** | | Felixstowe | Murder of step-daughter | **Hanged - Rushmere March 28th details IJ April 2nd** |
| Mar 26th IJ | 1785 | **John** | **Cone** | | Halesworth | Horse stealing | **Hanged - Rushmere April 9th** |
| Mar 30th BP | 1785 | Thomas | Jacobs | | Blakenham | Stealing a mare | presumed reprieved |
| July 23rd IJ | 1785 | **Thomas** | **Clark(from Yorkshire)** | | Yoxford | Shooting and Robbery | **Hanged - Rushmere July 30th details IJ August 6th** |

| Date of trial report | Year | Christian name | Surname | Age | Place offence committed | Crime | Outcome |
|---|---|---|---|---|---|---|---|
| July 23rd IJ | 1785 | Thomas | Carty(from Ireland) | | Yoxford | Shooting and Robbery | **Hanged - Rushmere July 30th** details IJ August 6th |
| July 23rd IJ | 1785 | John | Deane(from Ireland) | | Yoxford | Shooting and Robbery | **Hanged - Rushmere July 30th** details IJ August 6th |
| July 23rd IJ | 1785 | Robert | Woods | | | Stealing from a house | reprieved |
| July 23rd IJ | 1785 | Robert | Gooding | | Weybread | Stealing a cow | reprieved |
| Mar 25th IJ | 1786 | William | Last alias Denny | | Walton | Sheep stealing | **Hanged - Rushmere April 15th** |
| Mar 25th IJ | 1786 | James | Bantock | | Bacton | Stealing a mare | respited during His Majesty's Pleasure |
| Mar 25th IJ | 1786 | John | Williams | | Benhall | Robbery | **Hanged - Rushmere April 15th** |
| Mar 25th IJ | 1786 | Anthony | Bye | | | Sheep stealing | reprieved |
| Mar 25th IJ | 1786 | Simon | Starkey | | Heveningham | Sheep stealing | reprieved & later sent to Woolwich for transportation IJ March 24th 1787 |
| Mar 25th IJ | 1786 | William | Churchman | | Beccles | Stealing cows | reprieved and transported to New South Wales for 14 years in 1789 |
| Mar 25th IJ | 1786 | John | Brett alias Tregget | | West Bergholt | Horse stealing | reprieved & later sent to Woolwich for transportation IJ March 24th 1787 |
| Mar 25th IJ | 1786 | Thomas | Jacques | | Ufford | Horse stealing | reprieved: Later, convicted and transported for stealing a hog in 1791 |
| Mar 25th IJ | 1786 | William | Bennett | | Bardwell | Stealing a lamb | reprieved |
| Aug 12th IJ | 1786 | George | Sherman or Sharman | | Westerfield | Sheep stealing | reprieved |
| Aug 12th IJ | 1786 | John | Lockwood | | Bury | Robbery | reprieved |
| Aug 12th IJ | 1786 | William | Gowen | | Laxfield | Arson | Sentenced March 30th 1787. **Hanged - Rushmere April 21st 1787** |
| Mar 31st IJ | 1787 | Edward | Courtnell | | Tattingstone | Robbery | reprieved and transported to New South Wales for life in 1791 |
| Mar 31st IJ | 1787 | Isaac | Blomfield | | | Highway robbery | **Hanged - Rushmere April 21st** |

| Date of trial report | Year | Age | Christian name | Surname | Place offence committed | Crime | Outcome |
|---|---|---|---|---|---|---|---|
| Mar 3 1st IJ | 1787 | 26 | **Thomas** | **Hutchinson (or Hedgson)** | | Highway robbery | **Hanged - Rushmere April 21st confession IJ April 28th** |
| Mar 3 1st IJ | 1787 | | John | Kingsbury | Liston, Sudbury | Stealing a heifer | reprieved and transported to New South Wales for life in 1791 |
| Mar 3 1st IJ | 1787 | | John | Wharby | Lakenheath | Sheep stealing | reprieved |
| Mar 3 1st IJ | 1787 | | James | Weavers | Needham Market | Robbery | reprieved and transported to New South Wales for life in 1789 |
| Mar 3 1st IJ | 1787 | | John | Gosling | Dennington | Stealing a colt | reprieved and transported to New South Wales for life in 1791 |
| Mar 3 1st IJ | 1787 | | Robert | Sharman | Dunwich | Stealing a church bell | reprieved |
| Mar 3 1st IJ | 1787 | | William | Deaves | Felsham | Stealing a mare | reprieved and transported to New South Wales for life in 1791 |
| Mar 3 1st IJ | 1787 | | Henry | Cone | Halesworth | Robbery | reprieved and transported to New South Wales for life in 1789 |
| Aug 1st BP | 1787 | | **John** | **Mayes** | Blundeston | Burglary | **Hanged - Rushmere August 11th** |
| Aug 1st BP | 1787 | | **George** | **Chamberlain** | Blundeston | Burglary | **Hanged - Rushmere August 11th** |
| Aug 1st BP | 1787 | | **John** | **Barnes alias Davey alias Smith** | Blundeston | Burglary | **Hanged - Rushmere August 11th** details of fight in gaol IJ August 4th, details of execution IJ August 18th |
| Mar 29th IJ | 1788 | | Nathaniel | Lillie | Sudbury | Burglary | reprieved and transported to New South Wales for life 1789 |
| Mar 29th IJ | 1788 | | Stephen | Prike | Sudbury | Robbery | reprieved |
| Mar 29th IJ | 1788 | | William | Argent | Sudbury | Robbery | reprieved |
| Mar 29th IJ | 1788 | | John | Mays | | Horse stealing | reprieved |
| Mar 29th IJ | 1788 | | John | Wiseman | Cretingham | Robbery | reprieved and transported to New South Wales for life in 1789 |
| Mar 29th IJ | 1788 | | John | Levell | Tollesbury, Essex | Stealing a mare | reprieved and transported to New South Wales for life in 1789 |
| Mar 28th IJ | 1789 | | Isaac | Moyse | Kessingland | Stealing a mare | reprieved and transported to New South Wales in 1792 |

| Date of trial report | Year | Christian name | Surname | Age | Place offence committed | Crime | Outcome |
|---|---|---|---|---|---|---|---|
| Mar 28th IJ | 1789 | William alias Abraham | Mayhew | | Brent Eleigh | Robbery | Set to hang at Bury April 15th, respited one month BP April 8th, pardoned and sentenced to be transported for life to coast of Africa: BP June 17th   Actually sailed for New South Wales in 1791 |
| Mar 28th IJ | 1789 | John | Allington | | Ipswich gaol | Escaping gaol under sentence of transportation | reprieved and transported to New South Wales for life in 1789 |
| Aug 8th IJ | 1789 | **John** | **Dowsing** | 57 | Halesworth | Murder - Strangled wife | **Hanged - Rushmere August 5th** Reported IJ August 8th |
| Aug 8th IJ | 1789 | John | Hunter | | Tattingstone | Stealing a bull calf | reprieved - attempted gaol break reported IJ October 10th 1789 |
| Mar 27th IJ | 1790 | John | Lilley (a gipsy) | | Withersfield | Highway robbery | respited, reprieved and transported to New South Wales in 1791 |
| Mar 27th IJ | 1790 | Robert | Heron (a gipsy) | | Withersfield | Highway robbery | respited, presumed reprieved |
| Mar 27th IJ | 1790 | John | Rainham | | Lavenham | Highway robbery | respited, presumed reprieved |
| Mar 27th IJ | 1790 | John | Boreham | | Lavenham | Highway robbery | respited, presumed reprieved |
| Mar 27th IJ | 1790 | **William** | **Ranson** | | Lavenham | Burglary | **Hanged - Bury April 28th after twice respited** |
| Mar 27th IJ | 1790 | **John** | **Barton** | | Stansfield | House breaking | **Hanged - Bury April 8th** |
| Mar 27th IJ | 1790 | **Thomas** | **Browne** | | Stansfield | House breaking | **Hanged - Bury April 8th** |
| Mar 27th IJ | 1790 | **John** | **Southwell** | | On an army camp (Once postmaster of Saxmundham) | Sodomy | **Hanged - Rushmere April 3rd** |
| Mar 27th IJ | 1790 | **John** | **Smith** | | On an army camp | Sodomy | **Hanged - Rushmere April 3rd** |
| Mar 27th IJ | 1790 | **Francis** | **Mills** | | | Horse stealing | **Hanged - Rushmere April 3rd** |

| Date of trial report | Year | Christian name | Surname | Age | Place offence committed | Crime | Outcome |
|---|---|---|---|---|---|---|---|
| Mar 27th IJ | 1790 | Hezekiah | Sealie | | Chedburgh | Stealing a mare | reprieved - Hard labour 12 months |
| Mar 27th IJ | 1790 | Philip | Aldridge | | Cransford | Stealing a mare | reprieved and transported to New South Wales for 7 years in 1791 |
| Mar 27th IJ | 1790 | Henry | Burgess | | Halesworth | House breaking | reprieved and transported to New South Wales for 7 years in 1791  Attempted gaol break with 4 other prisoners before his trial, reported IJ January 30th 1790 |
| Mar 27th IJ | 1790 | Henry | Thurlow | | Stowmarket | Burglary | reprieved and transported to New South Wales for 7 years in 1791 |
| July 31st IJ | 1790 | Jonathan | Burrows | | Horham | Stealing a mare | reprieved and transported to New South Wales for 7 years in 1791 |
| July 31st IJ | 1790 | Rebecca | Smith | | Eye | Robbery | reprieved |
| Apr 2nd IJ | 1791 | Thomas | Nursey | | | Sheep stealing | reprieved and transported to New South Wales for 7 years in 1791 |
| Apr 2nd IJ | 1791 | James | Rayner | | Nayland | Stealing bankers notes | respited twice, transported to New South Wales for 7 years in 1791 |
| Aug 20th IJ | 1791 | Thomas | Harper | | Lakenheath | Murder of Thomas Briggs | reprieved |
| Apr 7th IJ | 1792 | Roger | Benstead Snr. | | Lakenheath | Murder of Thomas Briggs | **Hanged - Bury April 9th   hung in chains at Lakenheath** |
| Apr 7th IJ | 1792 | James | Mann | | Wickham Market | Highway robbery | Committed suicide in Ipswich gaol   Details BP April 11th |
| Apr 7th IJ | 1792 | Richard | Sealing | | Mildenhall | Stealing a mare | reprieved |
| Apr 7th IJ | 1792 | John | Batram alias Skipper | | | Stealing a mare | reprieved |
| Apr 7th IJ | 1792 | Thomas | Clark alias Martin | | Hertfordshire | Stealing a gelding | reprieved |
| Apr 7th IJ | 1792 | William | Eagle | | Newmarket | Stealing bank notes | reprieved |
| Aug 4th IJ | 1792 | Robert | Carman | | Halesworth | Stealing a purse and watch | reprieved |

| Date of trial report | Year | Christian name | Surname | Age | Place offence committed | Crime | Outcome |
|---|---|---|---|---|---|---|---|
| Mar 29th IJ | 1794 | John | Nichols | 59 | Fakenham Magna | Murder of Sarah Nichols (daughter) | Hanged - Bury March 26th and hung in chains Details: IJ March 29th |
| Mar 29th IJ | 1794 | Nathan | Nichols | 19 | Fakenham Magna | Murder of Sarah Nichols (sister) | Hanged - Bury March 26th and given to doctors for dissection Details: IJ March 29th |
| Mar 29th IJ | 1794 | Mary | Eady | | Lyndsey | Burglary | reprieved |
| Mar 29th IJ | 1794 | James | Gardener | | Saxted | Burglary | reprieved |
| Mar 29th IJ | 1794 | James | Adams | | Wickham Market | Stealing a gelding | reprieved |
| Mar 29th IJ | 1794 | Thomas | Merchant | | Hadleigh | Stealing a ewe | reprieved |
| Apr 4th IJ | 1795 | John | Bradfield | | Colkirk | Stealing five heifers | reprieved and transported to New South Wales for life in 1796 |
| Apr 4th IJ | 1795 | James | Harrax (or Horrex) | | Finborough | Stealing a ewe | reprieved and transported to New South Wales for 14 years in 1796 |
| Apr 4th IJ | 1795 | Miles | Mills | | | Returning early from transportation | reprieved and sent to Portsmouth for transportation to New South Wales in 1795 |
| Aug 1st IJ | 1795 | Charles | Blyth | 40 | Coddenham | Stealing a gelding | Hanged - Ipswich August 15th Details IJ August Aug 22nd |
| Aug 1st IJ | 1795 | James | Dosser | 33 | Woodbridge | Burglary | Hanged - Ipswich August 15th Details IJ August Aug 22nd |
| Aug 1st IJ | 1795 | William | Clarke | | Ipswich | Burglary | reprieved |
| Mar 23rd BP | 1796 | Thomas | Risby | | Cockfield | Stealing bread and cheese | reprieved |
| Mar 23rd BP | 1796 | Robert | Sturgeon | | Cockfield | Stealing bread and cheese | reprieved |
| Mar 23rd BP | 1796 | John | Partridge | | Stoke by Nayland | Stealing a ewe | reprieved |

| Date of trial report | Year | Christian name | Surname | Age | Place offence committed | Crime | Outcome |
|---|---|---|---|---|---|---|---|
| Mar 23rd BP | 1796 | John | Collins | | Stoke by Nayland | Stealing a ewe | reprieved |
| Mar 23rd BP | 1796 | James | Ventrice | | Bury | Stealing muslin | reprieved |
| Mar 23rd BP | 1796 | Robert | Bear | | Melford | Stealing clothing | reprieved |
| Mar 23rd BP | 1796 | Robert | Jones | | Woodbridge | Robbery | reprieved |
| Mar 23rd BP | 1796 | Jonathan | Kettle | | Bungay | Stealing 20 guineas | reprieved |
| July 20th BP | 1796 | **James** | **Copsey** | 26 | Cambridgeshire | Highway robbery | **Hanged - Bury August 10th after a respite of 7 days** |
| July 20th BP | 1796 | **Daniel** | **Burrows** | 24 | Stonham | Highway robbery | **Hanged - Bury August 10th after a respite of 7 days** |
| July 20th BP | 1796 | James | Cowell | | Woodbridge | Stealing a sheep | reprieved and transported to New South Wales for 7 years in 1801 |
| July 20th BP | 1796 | James | Green | | Woodbridge | Receiving sheep meat | sentence respited |
| Mar 29th BP | 1797 | John | Robinson | | Woolpit | Stealing 2 lambs | Was to be hanged April 12th but respited during His Majesty's Pleasure.   Had attempted to escape - BP March 22nd   Transported to New South Wales in 1802 |
| Mar 29th BP | 1797 | **William** | **Spurgin** | | Flixton | Horse stealing | **Hanged - Ipswich April 15th** |
| Mar 29th BP | 1797 | James | Gibson | | Laxfield | Stealing a sheep | reprieved and transported to New South Wales for 7 years in 1798 |
| Mar 29th BP | 1797 | John | Taylor | | | Stealing a bullock | reprieved and transported to New South Wales for 7 years in 1798 |
| Mar 29th BP | 1797 | John | King | | Ipswich | Highway robbery | reprieved and transported to New South Wales in 1798 |
| Mar 29th BP | 1797 | Diana | Parker | | | Stealing from a house | reprieved |
| Aug 16th BP | 1797 | **William** | **Powell** | 70 | | Sodomy | **Hanged - Bury August 30th** |
| Aug 16th BP | 1797 | Margaret | Catchpole | 35 | Ipswich | Horse stealing | reprieved, escaped from gaol - see August 1801 |
| Aug 16th BP | 1797 | George | Bidwell | | Ipswich | Stealing bank notes | reprieved |

| Date of trial report | Year | Christian name | Surname | Age | Place offence committed | Crime | Outcome |
|---|---|---|---|---|---|---|---|
| Aug 16th BP | 1797 | John | Hearn | | Great Cornard | Stealing a ram | reprieved |
| Mar 28th BP | 1798 | Edward | Bosworth | | Kentford | Assault on the highway | reprieved and transported 7 years |
| Mar 28th BP | 1798 | William | Borrett | 17 | Eyke | Stealing a lamb | reprieved - gaol 2 years |
| Mar 28th BP | 1798 | Mary | Syrett | | Beccles | Stealing from a house | reprieved - gaol 2 years |
| Mar 28th BP | 1798 | Elizabeth | Lacey | | Herringfleet | Stealing from a house | reprieved - gaol 2 years |
| Mar 28th BP | 1798 | Sarah | Barker | | | Stealing from a house | reprieved and transported to New South Wales for 7 years in 1801 |
| Mar 27th BP | 1799 | Phoebe | Syrett | | Beccles | Stealing from a house | reprieved |
| Mar 27th BP | 1799 | Richard | Nash | | Ipswich | Stealing 3 watches | reprieved |
| Mar 26th BP | 1800 | Edmund | Roberts (alias Hewett, alias Smith) | | Stratford | Horse stealing | deferred 10 days (Apr 9th), then respited |
| Mar 26th BP | 1800 | Thomas | Shop | | Ipswich | Burglary | Hanged - Ipswich April 19th |
| Mar 26th BP | 1800 | Sarah | Lloyd | 19 | Hadleigh | Theft (& arson) | Hanged - Bury St. Edmunds April 23rd Details BP April 30th |
| Mar 26th BP | 1800 | John | Wicks | | | Highway robbery | reprieved |
| Mar 26th BP | 1800 | John | Howlett/Howell | | Hinderclay | Shoplifting | reprieved |
| Mar 26th BP | 1800 | Barbara | Lambgerre | | | Stealing 6 guineas | |
| Mar 26th BP | 1800 | Benjamin | Blackwell | | Ipswich | Stealing from a house | reprieved |
| Mar 26th BP | 1800 | John | Carss | | Ipswich | Stealing from a house | reprieved |
| Aug 6th BP | 1800 | James Orman | Clark | 23 | Halesworth | Housebreaking | respite of 10 days (BP Aug 27th), further month respite (BP Sep 3rd) |
| Aug 6th BP | 1800 | Margaret | Catchpole | 38 | Ipswich | Horse stealing | reprieved for second time having escaped from Ipswich gaol - transportation to New South Wales for 7 years in 1801 |
| Apr 1st BP | 1801 | Simon | Payne (Snr.) | | Walton | Receiving | reprieved - transportation |

| Date of trial report | Year | Christian name | Surname | Age | Place offence committed | Crime | Outcome |
|---|---|---|---|---|---|---|---|
| Apr 1st BP | 1801 | Henry | Warren | 46 | Walsham-le-Willows | Sheep stealing | **Hanged – Bury St. Edmunds April 8th** |
| Apr 1st BP | 1801 | Thomas | O(a)gles | | Copdock | Burglary | **Hanged – Ipswich April 11th** Reported IJ April 18th |
| Apr 1st BP | 1801 | Simon | Payne (Jnr.) | | Walton | Burglary | **Hanged – Ipswich April 11th** Reported IJ April 18th |
| Mar 25th BP | 1801 | Edward | Cureton | | Copdock | Burglary | reprieved and transported for life to New South Wales in 1802 |
| Mar 25th BP | 1801 | Thomas | Andlezak | | Copdock | Burglary | reprieved and transported for life to New South Wales in 1802 |
| Mar 25th BP | 1801 | Peter | Smith | | Thetford | Horse stealing | reprieved |
| Mar 25th BP | 1801 | John | Barton | | Newmarket | Highway robbery | reprieved |
| Mar 25th BP | 1801 | J | Mcnaughton | | Newmarket | Highway robbery | reprieved |
| Mar 25th BP | 1801 | William | Denton | | Bury | Firing a pistol at Wm. Carter | reprieved and transported for life to New South Wales 1802 |
| Mar 25th BP | 1801 | Isaac | Miller | | Melford | Robbery | reprieved |
| Mar 25th BP | 1801 | John | Bealing | | Spexhall | Robbery | reprieved and transported for life to New South Wales 1803 |
| Apr 1st BP | 1801 | James | Powell | | Barton Mills | Stealing 4 casks of liquor | reprieved |
| Apr 1st BP | 1801 | Lawrence | Hand | | Brockford | Stealing money | reprieved |
| July 29th BP | 1801 | William | Baldwin | 45 | Ipswich | Highway robbery | **Hanged – Ipswich August 15th** Details BP August 19th |
| July 29th BP | 1801 | James | Arnold | | Debenham | Sheep stealing | reprieved |
| July 29th BP | 1801 | John | Hardingham | | Laxfield | Stealing a calf | reprieved |
| Mar 31st BP | 1802 | John | Read (alias Oxer) | 25 | Yaxley | Housebreaking | **Hanged – Ipswich April 17th** Details IJ April 24th |
| Mar 31st BP | 1802 | Thomas | Keeley | 22 | Thrandeston | Housebreaking | **Hanged – Ipswich April 17th** Details IJ April 24th |
| Mar 31st BP | 1802 | Jonathan | Turner | | Edwardstone | Stealing a mare | reprieved |

| Date of trial report | Year | Christian name | Surname | Age | Place offence committed | Crime | Outcome |
|---|---|---|---|---|---|---|---|
| Aug 11th BP | 1802 | William | Gibbs | 19 | Kesgrave | Highway robbery | reprieved - Details BP Aug 11th |
| Mar 30th BP | 1803 | Hannah | Williams | | Wickhambrook | Housebreaking | respite (Apr 13th) commuted to transportation (BP Nov. 9th) to New South Wales |
| Mar 30th BP | 1803 | Richard | Brown | | Wickhambrook | Housebreaking | Hanged - Bury St. Edmunds April 13th Details BP April 20th |
| Mar 30th BP | 1803 | John | Sowter | | Westhall | Stealing a mare | reprieved |
| Mar 30th BP | 1803 | Nicholas | Sustenance | | Gorleston | Highway robbery | reprieved |
| Mar 30th BP | 1803 | Samuel | Farrer | | Gorleston | Highway robbery | reprieved |
| Mar 30th BP | 1803 | James | Harvey | | | Burglary | reprieved |
| Mar 30th BP | 1803 | John | Gidney | | Boston, Lincs | Horse stealing | reprieved |
| Aug 3rd BP | 1803 | Thomas | Ling | | Stradishall | Arson | respite (Aug 17th, day of intended execution) |
| Aug 3rd BP | 1803 | Jonathan | Pollard | | | House breaking | reprieved |
| Aug 3rd BP | 1803 | William | Corner | | | House breaking | reprieved |
| Aug 3rd BP | 1803 | Samuel | Knivett alias Neville | | Ipswich | Assault and Highway robbery | reprieved |
| Aug 3rd BP | 1803 | Daniel | Kennedy | | Ipswich | Assault and Highway robbery | reprieved |
| Aug 3rd BP | 1803 | James | Dobbin | | Rushmere | Stealing a mare | reprieved |
| Aug 3rd BP | 1803 | Robert | Copping alias Mason | | Essex | Stealing a mare | reprieved |
| Mar 28th BP | 1804 | Lionel | Lee | 35 | Combs | Housebreaking | Hanged - Ipswich April 14th Reported IJ April 21st |
| Mar 28th BP | 1804 | Elizabeth | Elliott | | Great Blakenham | House breaking | reprieved |
| Mar 28th BP | 1804 | James | Block | | | Stealing from a house | reprieved - may be the same person as appears in July 1812 |
| Mar 28th BP | 1804 | Edward | Allen | | Ipswich | Stealing a mare | reprieved |

| Date of trial report | Year | Christian name | Surname | Age | Place offence committed | Crime | Outcome |
|---|---|---|---|---|---|---|---|
| Aug 1st BP | 1804 | Benjamin Walter | Gunn | | Stowupland | Stealing a cow | reprieved |
| Aug 1st BP | 1804 | William | Arnold | | Stowupland | Stealing a cow | reprieved |
| Aug 10th IJ | 1805 | William | Holmes | 46 | Melton | Rape of a child under 10 | **Hanged - Ipswich August 24th** Details IJ August 31st |
| Aug 7th BP | 1805 | William | English | | | Horse stealing | reprieved |
| Aug 7th BP | 1805 | R | Littlewood alias Smith | | | Horse stealing | reprieved |
| Aug 7th BP | 1805 | James | Frost | | | Horse stealing | reprieved |
| Aug 7th BP | 1805 | James | Lucas | | | Sheep stealing | reprieved |
| Apr 2nd BP | 1806 | George | Christian | 26 | Woodbridge | Horse-stealing | **Hanged - Ipswich April 12th** Details BP April 16th/IJ April 19th |
| Apr 2nd BP | 1806 | Shadrack | Dewey | 30 | Ipswich | Shooting at Capt. Brooke | **Hanged - Ipswich April 12th** Details BP April 16th/IJ April 19th |
| Apr 2nd BP | 1806 | Dyson | Post | | Thetford | Altering a bank note | respite until May 14th, then further respite, reprieved and transported for 7 years (BP August 6th) to New South Wales |
| Apr 2nd BP | 1806 | John | Smith | | Needham | Burglary | reprieved |
| Apr 2nd BP | 1806 | Richard | Fletcher | | Ipswich | Stealing 9 watches | reprieved, 2 years House of Correction |
| Apr 2nd BP | 1806 | Benjamin | Colley | | Ipswich | Stealing 9 watches | reprieved, 2 years House of Correction |
| Apr 2nd BP | 1806 | William | Shaw | | Ipswich | Highway robbery | reprieved, 2 years House of Correction |
| Apr 2nd BP | 1806 | John | Wallace | | Ipswich | Highway robbery | reprieved |
| Aug 17th IJ | 1806 | Henry | Deighton | | Great Thurlow | Housebreaking | reprieved & transported for life |
| Aug 17th IJ | 1806 | John | Hurst | | Stradishall | Sheep stealing | reprieved and transported for life to New South Wales in 1809 |
| Aug 17th IJ | 1806 | Thomas | Hurst | | Stradishall | Sheep stealing | reprieved |
| Aug 17th IJ | 1806 | William | Parsons alias Sparke | | Lawshall | Horse stealing | reprieved |

| Date of trial report | Year | Christian name | Surname | Age | Place offence committed | Crime | Outcome |
|---|---|---|---|---|---|---|---|
| Aug 17th IJ | 1806 | William | Burrell | | Ipswich | Horse stealing | reprieved (Aug 30th) |
| Aug 17th IJ | 1806 | Luke | Castle | 21 | Stradishall | Burglary with violence | **Hanged - Bury St. Edmunds August 27th** Details BP August 13th, IJ August 30th |
| Aug 17th IJ | 1806 | Samuel | Wheeler | 18 | Stradishall | Burglary with violence | **Hanged - Bury St. Edmunds August 27th** Details BP August 13th, IJ August 30th |
| Aug 17th IJ | 1806 | Miles | Rayner | 57 | Ipswich | Stealing a mare | **Hanged - Ipswich August 30th** |
| Mar 25th BP | 1807 | Robert | Clark(e) | 40 | Bury | Forgery of bank-notes | **Hanged - Bury St. Edmunds April 8th** Details BP April 15th, confession IJ April 11th |
| Mar 25th BP | 1807 | John | Skelton | | Glemsford | Stealing a ewe | reprieved |
| Mar 25th BP | 1807 | John William | Smith | | Heveningham | Stealing a mare (from his grandfather) | reprieved |
| July 29th BP | 1807 | James | Notley | | Dalham | Sheep stealing | reprieved at last minute    Details BP August 12th  Transported for life to New South Wales in 1810 |
| Apr 2nd IJ | 1808 | William | Turner | 19 | Rushford Lodge | Sheep stealing | reprieved and transported for life to New South Wales in 1810 |
| Apr 2nd IJ | 1808 | Benjamin | Wright | 29 | Witnesham | Theft | reprieved and transported for life to New South Wales in 1810 |
| Apr 2nd IJ | 1808 | John | Mayes (father) | 46 | Thornham Magna | Housebreaking | reprieved and transported for 14 years to New South Wales in 1811 |
| Apr 2nd IJ | 1808 | George | Mayes (son) | 14 | Thornham Magna | Housebreaking | reprieved |
| Apr 2nd IJ | 1808 | Robert | Ge(a)rard | | Thornham Magna | Housebreaking | reprieved and transported for 14 years to New South Wales in 1811 |
| Apr 2nd IJ | 1808 | George | Ratcliffe | 41 | Bury | Stabbing work-house master | reprieved - transportation, 7 yrs. Details BP March 30th |
| Aug 17th BP | 1808 | Joseph | Arnold | | Ipswich | Housebreaking | reprieved and transported for life to New South Wales in 1810 |

| Date of trial report | Year | Christian name | Surname | Age | Place offence committed | Crime | Outcome |
|---|---|---|---|---|---|---|---|
| Apr 1st IJ | 1809 | Jesse | Baker | | Elmswell | Stole a watch | reprieved |
| Apr 1st IJ | 1809 | William | Lambert | | Ixworth | Stealing liquors | reprieved and transported for life to New South Wales in 1810 |
| Apr 1st IJ | 1809 | Richer | Smith | | Huntingfield | Stealing a heifer | reprieved |
| Aug 2nd BP | 1809 | **Matthew** | **Riley/Reilly (soldier)** | 27 | Ipswich | Murder of Robt. Howe | **Hanged - Ipswich July 31st. Details: BP August 2nd** |
| Aug 2nd BP | 1809 | **John** | **Dogharty (soldier)** | 22 | Ipswich | Murder of Robt. Howe | **Hanged - Ipswich July 31st. Details: BP August 2nd** |
| Aug 2nd BP | 1809 | Thomas | Murrells | | Stoke by Nayland | Sheep stealing | reprieved and transported for life to New South Wales in 1811 |
| Aug 2nd BP | 1809 | Robert | Harvey | | Baylham | Stealing a calf | reprieved |
| Aug 2nd BP | 1809 | Henry | Clark (or Clack) | | Laxfield | Stealing from a house | reprieved and transported for 14 years to New South Wales in 1811 |
| Mar 31st IJ | 1810 | **James** | **Crow (alias Fyson)** | 18 | Mildenhall | Highway robbery | **Hanged - Bury St. Edmunds April 11th** Details of execution IJ April 14th |
| Mar 31st IJ | 1810 | Charles | Kent | 22 | Mildenhall | Highway robbery | reprieved and transported for life to New South Wales in 1811 |
| Mar 31st IJ | 1810 | William | Rose | | Hunston | Stealing a lamb | reprieved |
| Mar 31st IJ | 1810 | Bridget | Crack | | Bury | Stealing calico | reprieved and transported for life to New South Wales in 1812 |
| Mar 31st IJ | 1810 | Thomas | Brown | | Wangford | Stealing clothes | reprieved |
| Mar 31st IJ | 1810 | Charles | Curtis | | Thwaite | Horse stealing | reprieved |
| Mar 31st IJ | 1810 | Harriet | Barker | | Hasketon | Stealing bank notes | reprieved |
| Aug 25th IJ | 1810 | Phoebe | Harvey | | Tannington | Stealing two £10 notes | reprieved |
| Apr 6th IJ | 1811 | Jonathan | Turner | | Ipswich | Horse stealing | reprieved |
| Apr 6th IJ | 1811 | John | Avis | | Rougham | Sheep stealing | reprieved |
| Apr 6th IJ | 1811 | William | Caley | | Falkenham | Stealing a lamb | reprieved |
| Apr 6th IJ | 1811 | William | Burling | | Kentford | Stealing clothing | reprieved |
| Apr 6th IJ | 1811 | Robert | Abbott | | Framlingham | Stealing a purse | reprieved |

| Date of trial report | Year | Christian name | Surname | Age | Place offence committed | Crime | Outcome |
|---|---|---|---|---|---|---|---|
| Aug 17th IJ | 1811 | John | Rose | | Bredfield | Burglary | reprieved and transported for life to New South Wales in 1812 |
| Aug 17th IJ | 1811 | James | Jessup | | Bredfield | Burglary | reprieved and transported for life to New South Wales in 1812 |
| Mar 28th IJ | 1812 | Edward/ Edmund | **Thrower** | 58 | Cratfield | Murder | **Hanged - Ipswich March 23rd** Details IJ March 28th |
| Mar 28th IJ | 1812 | **John** | **Smith** | 39 | Cookley | Murder of his child | **Hanged - Ipswich March 23rd** Details IJ March 28th |
| Mar 28th IJ | 1812 | **Elizabeth** | **Smith** | 27 | Cookley | Murder of her step-child | **Hanged - Ipswich March 23rd** Details IJ March 28th |
| Mar 28th IJ | 1812 | **John** | **Took** | 40 | Melton | Rape of his daughter | **Hanged - Ipswich April 11th** Details IJ April 18th |
| Mar 28th IJ | 1812 | Mary | Marjoram | | Badingham | Arson | reprieved and transported for 7 years to New South Wales in 1813 |
| Mar 28th IJ | 1812 | *James* | *Boyd* | | | *Stealing a gelding* | *Possibly death recorded, reprieved and transported for life to New South Wales 1812* |
| Mar 28th IJ | 1812 | John Flora | Wilkinson alias Read | | Ipswich | Stealing from a house | reprieved |
| Mar 28th IJ | 1812 | William | Glazier | | apprehended in Sudbury for crime committed in Surrey | Stealing a mare | reprieved |
| Mar 28th IJ | 1812 | Henry | Neale | | Tuddenham | Sheep stealing | reprieved and transported for life to New South Wales in 1815 |
| Mar 28th IJ | 1812 | James | Clarke | | Tuddenham | Sheep stealing | reprieved and transported for life to New South Wales in 1813 |

| Date of trial report | Year | Christian name | Surname | Age | Place offence committed | Crime | Outcome |
|---|---|---|---|---|---|---|---|
| Aug 1st IJ At this court only 11 cases were tried, but 8 secured death sentences | 1812 | William | Finch | | Melford | Burglary | reprieved and transported for life to New South Wales in 1813 |
| Aug 1st IJ | 1812 | John | Cant | | Sudbury | Sheep stealing | reprieved and transported for life to New South Wales in 1813 |
| Aug 1st IJ | 1812 | John | Bareham | | Sudbury | Sheep stealing | reprieved and transported for life to New South Wales in 1813 |
| Aug 1st IJ | 1812 | Joseph | Bonney | | Sudbury | Burglary | reprieved and transported for life to New South Wales in 1813 |
| Aug 1st IJ | 1812 | James | Block | | Charsfield | Breaking & entering | reprieved and transported for life to New South Wales in 1812 |
| Aug 1st IJ | 1812 | Barzillai | Bensley | | Westleton | Breaking & entering | reprieved and transported for life to New South Wales in 1812 |
| Aug 1st IJ | 1812 | Jane | Folkard | | Dunwich | Stealing £35 | reprieved and transported for 7 years to New South Wales in 1813 |
| Aug 1st IJ | 1812 | John | Ablett | | Great Bealings | Horse stealing | reprieved and transported for life to New South Wales in 1812 |
| Apr 3rd IJ | 1813 | **Ann** | **Arnold** | 29 | Spexhall | Murder – throwing her child into a pond | **Hanged – Ipswich March 29th** Details:  SC March 29th/ BP March 31st/IJ April 3rd |
| Apr 3rd IJ | 1813 | Mary | Todd | 18 | Wickham Skeith | House breaking | presumed reprieved |
| Apr 3rd IJ | 1813 | John | Spink | 30 | Wickham Skeith | Burglary | reprieved and transported for life to New South Wales in 1813 |
| Apr 3rd IJ | 1813 | John | Garrod (or Garrard) | 25 | Wickham Skeith | Burglary | reprieved and transported for life to New South Wales in 1813 |

| Date of trial report | Year | Christian name | Surname | Age | Place offence committed | Crime | Outcome |
|---|---|---|---|---|---|---|---|
| Apr 3rd IJ | 1813 | Charles | Nunn | 39 | Wickham Skeith | Burglary | reprieved and transported for life to New South Wales in 1813 |
| Apr 3rd IJ | 1813 | John | Hayward | 29 | Wickham Skeith | Burglary | reprieved and transported for life to New South Wales in 1813 |
| Apr 3rd IJ | 1813 | John | Cook | 27 | Beyton | Stealing 2 bullocks | reprieved and transported for life to New South Wales in 1813 |
| Apr 3rd IJ | 1813 | Robert | Wood | 29 | Beyton | Stealing 2 bullocks | reprieved and transported for life to New South Wales in 1813 |
| Apr 3rd IJ | 1813 | Richard | Sculthorpe | | Sudbury | Stealing a mare | reprieved and transported for life to New South Wales in 1813 |
| Apr 3rd IJ | 1813 | William | Callow alias Sturgeon | 22 | Hethersett | Horse stealing | reprieved and transported for life to New South Wales in 1813 |
| Aug 21st IJ | 1813 | James | Abbott alias Scofield | | Chelsworth | Sheep stealing | reprieved and transported for life to New South Wales in 1814 |
| Aug 21st IJ | 1813 | Nathaniel | Lilly | | Stanstead | Burglary | reprieved |
| Aug 21st IJ | 1813 | Robert | Ford | | Bredfield | Stealing a mare | reprieved and transported for life to New South Wales in 1814 |
| Aug 21st IJ | 1813 | Maria | Rackham | | Flixton | Sacrilege | reprieved |
| Mar 26th IJ | 1814 | Maurice | Griffin | 17 (or 20) | Woodbridge | Murder | **Hanged - Ipswich March 28th** Execution reported IJ April 2nd |
| Mar 26th IJ | 1814 | Mary | Gibbs | 23 | Hollesley | Murder of her bastard child | **Hanged - Ipswich March 28th** Execution reported IJ April 2nd |
| Aug 6th/13th IJ | 1814 | George | Maulkin or Marltin | 24 | Ixworth | Unnatural offence (bestiality with a mare) | **Hanged - Bury St. Edmunds August 24th** Details IJ August 27th |
| Aug 6th/13th IJ | 1814 | Thomas | Wright | | Lowestoft | Stealing a mare | reprieved and transported for life to New South Wales in 1815 |
| Apr 5th BP | 1815 | Sarah | Woodward | 25 | Frostenden | Murder of her bastard child | **Hanged - Ipswich April 3rd** Trial report BP April 3rd |

| Date of trial report | Year | Christian name | Surname | Age | Place offence committed | Crime | Outcome |
|---|---|---|---|---|---|---|---|
| Apr 5th BP | 1815 | Samuel | Brunning | | Great Waldingfield | Stealing a lamb | reprieved |
| Apr 5th BP | 1815 | John | Smith | | Lowestoft | Stealing a pony | reprieved |
| Apr 5th BP | 1815 | John | Allen | | Ipswich | Stealing a sheep | reprieved |
| July 26th BP | 1815 | Elizabeth or Mary | Wooltorton | 49 | North Cove | Murder of an infant | **Hanged – Ipswich July 25th after deferred a day** Details: BP July 26th |
| Mar 30th IJ | 1816 | William | Porter | | St. Andrew Ilketshall | Stealing a mare | reprieved |
| Mar 30th IJ | 1816 | William | Lines | | Framlingham | Stealing 3 lambs | reprieved |
| Mar 30th IJ | 1816 | Joseph | Cone | | Lowestoft | Stealing a sheep | reprieved but later transported to New South Wales for 7 years for stealing 5 hogs in Lowestoft in 1822 |
| Mar 30th IJ | 1816 | James | Mutton | | Lowestoft | Stealing a sheep | reprieved |
| Mar 30th IJ | 1816 | James | Barber | | Blundeston | Stealing a sheep | reprieved |
| Apr 3rd BP | 1816 | William | Green | | Lavenham | Sheep stealing | Left for execution but reprieved (BP April 17th) and transported for life to New South Wales in 1816. |
| Apr 3rd BP | 1816 | William | Smith | | Clare | Stealing a gelding | reprieved and transported for life to New South Wales in 1816 |
| Apr 3rd BP | 1816 | William | Wells | | between Stowmarket & Bury | Highway robbery & assault | reprieved and transported for life to New South Wales in 1816 |
| Apr 3rd BP | 1816 | John | Markall | | between Stowmarket & Bury | Highway robbery & assault | reprieved |
| Apr 3rd BP | 1816 | James | Tyler | | Newmarket | burglary | reprieved |
| Apr 3rd BP | 1816 | John | Smith | | Cockfield | Stealing cloth | reprieved and transported for life to New South Wales in 1816 |

| Date of trial report | Year | Christian name | Surname | Age | Place offence committed | Crime | Outcome |
|---|---|---|---|---|---|---|---|
| Apr 3rd BP | 1816 | William | Cardy | | Bures | Sheep stealing | reprieved and sentenced to 2 years imprisonment |
| Apr 3rd BP | 1816 | Edward | Everitt | | Bures | Sheep stealing | reprieved    Possibly he is the Edward Everit who was transported for 7 years to Van Diemen's Land in 1820 for stealing wheat at Assington |
| Aug 17th IJ | 1816 | **Joseph** | **Bugg** | 26 | Martlesham | Setting fire to a barn | **Hanged – Ipswich April 24th** |
| Aug 17th IJ | 1816 | James | Pleasants | 15 | Lawshall | Arson | reprieved |
| Aug 17th IJ | 1816 | George | Young | | Bury | Forgery | reprieved and transported for life to New South Wales in 1816 |
| Aug 17th IJ | 1816 | George | Edwards | | Bury | Forgery | reprieved and transported for life to New South Wales in 1817 |
| Apr 5th IJ | 1817 | Samuel | Rayner | | Thetford | Robbery | reprieved and transported for life to New South Wales in 1817 |
| Apr 5th IJ | 1817 | Thomas | Knott | | Thrandeston | Breaking into a barn | reprieved and sentenced to 2 years imprisonment |
| Apr 5th IJ | 1817 | George | Ellet | | Bradwell | Stealing cheeses | reprieved and sentenced to 1 year imprisonment |
| Apr 5th IJ | 1817 | Mary | Neale | | Tuddenham | Stealing flour | reprieved |
| Apr 5th IJ | 1817 | William | Neale | | Tuddenham | Stealing flour | reprieved |
| Apr 5th IJ | 1817 | William | Wakeling | | Sudbury | Stealing sheep | reprieved - escaped from gaol    Details IJ April 20th/SC April 26th   Recaptured and transported for life to New South Wales in 1817 |
| Aug 9th IJ | 1817 | Robert | Bane | 31 | Ilketshall St. Lawrence | Burglary | reprieved |
| Aug 9th IJ | 1817 | Benjamin | Sharman | 33 | Ilketshall St. Lawrence | Burglary | reprieved and transported for 7 years to New South Wales in 1818 |
| Aug 9th IJ | 1817 | James | English | | Wattisfield | Burglary | reprieved |
| Aug 9th IJ | 1817 | Thomas | Watson | | Wattisfield | Burglary | reprieved |

| Date of trial report | Year | Christian name | Surname | Age | Place offence committed | Crime | Outcome |
|---|---|---|---|---|---|---|---|
| Aug 9th IJ | 1817 | Edward | Woodroffe | 22 | Mildenhall | Horse stealing | reprieved |
| Aug 9th IJ | 1817 | Robert | Youngs | 17 | Downham Market | Horse stealing | reprieved |
| Aug 9th IJ | 1817 | Joseph | Bredfield | 14 | Eye | House breaking | reprieved |
| Aug 9th IJ | 1817 | John | Richardson | 32 | East Bergholt | Sheep stealing | reprieved and transported for 14 years to New South Wales in 1818 |
| Aug 9th IJ | 1817 | James | Sage | 24 | East Bergholt | Felony - stole a watch | reprieved |
| Aug 9th IJ | 1817 | Joseph | Bullen | 21 | Metfield | Felony - stole a watch | IJ Says he was guilty, SC says *no true bill* . IJ says he was reprieved - probably the same Joseph Bullen who was transported in 1828 for a burglary committed in Metfield |
| Mar 28th/ Apr 4th SC | 1818 | John | Smith alias Suttle | 21 | Hadleigh | Burglary | reprieved and transported for life to New South Wales in 1818 |
| Mar 28th/ Apr 4th SC | 1818 | John | Downing | 21 | Bradfield St. George | Burglary | reprieved |
| Mar 28th/ Apr 4th SC | 1818 | Mingay | Rampling | 21 | Brandon | Burglary | reprieved and transported for life to New South Wales in 1818 |
| Mar 28th/ Apr 4th SC | 1818 | Jonathan | Sawyer | 18 | Framsden | Burglary | reprieved and transported for life to New South Wales in 1818 Details SC April 4th |
| Mar 28th/ Apr 4th SC | 1818 | James | Skinner | 19 | Marlesford | Burglary | reprieved |
| Mar 28th/ Apr 4th SC | 1818 | Stephen | Peck | 20 | Eye | Burglary | reprieved |
| Mar 28th/ Apr 4th SC | 1818 | William | Vickers or Pickers | 18 | Higham | Burglary | reprieved |
| Mar 28th/ Apr 4th SC | 1818 | James | El(e)y | 21 | Barton Place (Barton Parva) | Feloniously stealing | reprieved and transported for life to New South Wales in 1818 |

| Date of trial report | Year | Christian name | Surname | Age | Place offence committed | Crime | Outcome |
|---|---|---|---|---|---|---|---|
| Mar 28th/ Apr 4th SC | 1818 | Robert | Hoskins alias Harlett | 28 | Thelnetham | Horse stealing | reprieved |
| Mar 28th/ Apr 4th SC | 1818 | Stephen | Cook | 18 | Ipswich | Horse stealing | reprieved |
| Aug 1st SC | 1818 | **John** | **Bendale** | 30 | Thetford | House breaking | **Hanged - Bury St. Edmunds August 12th** Details SC August 15th |
| Aug 1st SC | 1818 | William | Flowers | 24 | Thetford | House breaking | reprieved |
| Aug 1st SC | 1818 | William | Selsby | 31 | Gislingham | Stealing 3 heifers | reprieved and transported for life to New South Wales in 1818 |
| Aug 1st SC | 1818 | James | Mowser | 34 | Cratfield | Burglary | reprieved and transported for life to New South Wales in 1819 |
| Apr 7th BP | 1819 | Mark | Blade | 40 | Brandon | Stealing £10 | reprieved |
| Apr 7th BP | 1819 | John | Webb | 14 | Exning | Arson | reprieved |
| Apr 7th BP | 1819 | Henry | Flack | 17 | Hilgay | Stealing a cow | reprieved |
| Apr 7th BP | 1819 | James | Tyler | 43 | Sudbury | Burglary | reprieved |
| Apr 7th BP | 1819 | Thomas | Foulger | 23 | Beyton | Stealing a ewe | reprieved and transported for life to New South Wales in 1819 |
| Apr 7th BP | 1819 | Elizabeth | Crawford | 23 | Bury | Stealing cloth | reprieved |
| Apr 7th BP | 1819 | John (or James) | Mayhew | | Newmarket | Stealing cloth | reprieved and transported for life to New South Wales in 1819 |
| Apr 7th BP | 1819 | William | Hardy | 22 | Thorpe Morieux | Stealing corn | reprieved and transported for life to New South Wales in 1819 |
| Apr 7th BP | 1819 | George | Smith | 28 | Theberton | Stealing a pony | reprieved |
| Apr 7th BP | 1819 | James | Johnson | 25 | Spexhall | Highway robbery | reprieved (He was blind) |
| Apr 7th BP | 1819 | John | Nicholds | 38 | Spexhall | Highway robbery | reprieved (He had a wooden leg) |
| Apr 7th BP | 1819 | Robert | Nunn | 24 | Huntingfield | Stealing money | reprieved |
| Apr 7th BP | 1819 | Charles | Rayner | 19 (or 21) | Wortham | Stealing a pony | reprieved  BP April 21st |

| Date of trial report | Year | Christian name | Surname | Age | Place offence committed | Crime | Outcome |
|---|---|---|---|---|---|---|---|
| Apr 7th BP | 1819 | James | Baldwin | 20 | Playford | House breaking | reprieved   Convicted in 1821 of a theft in Little Bealings and transported to Van Diemen's Land for 7 years |
| Apr 7th BP | 1819 | William | Syrett alias Robert Sayer | 21 | Bury | Forging a cheque | reprieved   Details SC April 3rd Transported for life to New South Wales in 1819 |
| Apr 7th BP | 1819 | William | Neave | 52 | Friston | Robbery | reprieved   BP April 21st |
| Apr 7th BP | 1819 | Thomas | Death | 40 | Bramford | Sheep stealing | reprieved and transported for life to New South Wales in 1819 |
| Apr 7th BP | 1819 | Robert | Harvey | 28 | Bramford | Sheep stealing | reprieved and transported for life to New South Wales in 1819 |
| Apr 7th BP | 1819 | Joseph | Webb | 48 | Bentley | Firing a pistol & theft | reprieved April 21st BP Details SC April 3rd |
| Apr 7th BP | 1819 | John Sterry | Baker | 22 | Wortham | Stealing a pony | reprieved   BP April 21st |
| Apr 7th BP | 1819 | **Joshua** | **Ranson** | 22 | Whitton | Housebreaking | **Hanged - Ipswich April 17th Details BP April 7th & 21st** |
| Apr 7th BP | 1819 | **William** | **Hillyard** | 33 | Whitton | Housebreaking | **Hanged - Ipswich April 17th Details BP April 7th & 21st** |
| Apr 7th BP | 1819 | **Henry** | **Laws** | 31 | Whitton | Housebreaking | **Hanged - Ipswich April 17th Details BP April 7th & 21st** |
| Aug 7th IJ | 1819 | John | Wells | 40 | Lackford | Stealing a pony | reprieved on condition of being transported for life   Details SC August 7th Transported for life to New South Wales in 1820 |
| Aug 7th IJ | 1819 | Isaac | Marrington alias Eaton | 36 | Elmswell & Woolpit | Burglary | reprieved on condition of being transported for life   Details SC August 7th  Probably the same Isaac Eaton who was transported to New South Wales for life for stealing a pony at Bardwell in 1823 |

| Date of trial report | Year | Christian name | Surname | Age | Place offence committed | Crime | Outcome |
|---|---|---|---|---|---|---|---|
| Aug 7th IJ | 1819 | John | Cook | 34 | Thornham | Burglary | reprieved on condition of being transported for life    Details SC August 7th    Transported for life to New South Wales in 1819 |
| Aug 14th IJ | 1819 | Thomas | Briggs | 24 | Bramfield | Burglary | reprieved on condition of being transported for life    Details SC August 14th    Transported for 7 years to New South Wales in 1819 |
| Apr 5th BP | 1820 | John | Wales | | Ipswich | Rape | Details BP April 5th  Petition sent to His Majesty BP April 12th   Respited BP April 19th |
| Apr 5th BP | 1820 | James | King | | Boxford | Burglary | reprieved and transported to New South Wales for life in 1820 |
| Apr 5th BP | 1820 | James | Thompson | | Mildenhall | Stealing a gelding | reprieved |
| Apr 5th BP | 1820 | John | Flack | | Little Whelnetham | House breaking | reprieved and transported for life to Van Diemen's Land in 1820 |
| Apr 5th BP | 1820 | John | East | | Cockfield | Highway robbery | reprieved |
| Apr 5th BP | 1820 | John | Austin | | Cockfield | Highway robbery | reprieved and transported to New South Wales for life in 1820 |
| Apr 5th BP | 1820 | John | Bennett | | Horningsheath | Burglary | reprieved |
| Apr 5th BP | 1820 | Elizabeth | Harald | | Bury | Burglary | reprieved |
| Apr 5th BP | 1820 | Isaac | Wordley | | Glemsford | Sheep stealing | reprieved and transported to New South Wales for life in 1820 |
| Apr 5th BP | 1820 | John | Wordley | | Glemsford | Sheep stealing | reprieved |
| Apr 5th BP | 1820 | Susan | Burton | | Rougham | Stealing a lamb | reprieved |
| Apr 5th BP | 1820 | Thomas | Hurn | | Bungay | Burglary | reprieved and transported to New South Wales for life in 1820 |
| Apr 5th BP | 1820 | James | Plumb | | East Bergholt | House breaking | reprieved and transported to New South Wales for life in 1820 |
| Apr 5th BP | 1820 | Matthew | Newell | | East Bergholt | House breaking | reprieved |

| Date of trial report | Year | Christian name | Surname | Age | Place offence committed | Crime | Outcome |
|---|---|---|---|---|---|---|---|
| Apr 5th BP | 1820 | Benjamin | Bunn | | Wenhaston | House breaking | respited BP April 12th   Had been acquitted in case at previous Assize where Thomas Briggs was found guilty.  Transported for life to New South Wales 1820 |
| Apr 5th BP | 1820 | William | Foreman | | Wenhaston | House breaking | reprieved |
| Apr 5th BP | 1820 | William | Calver | | Wenhaston | House breaking | reprieved |
| July 29th IJ | 1820 | Thomas | Bantock | | Badwell Ash | Stealing a cow | reprieved   Possibly the same Thomas Bantock transported for life to New South Wales in 1828 for stealing a heifer at Hawstead |
| July 29th IJ | 1820 | James | Curtis | | Culpho | Burglary | reprieved    May be the same James Curtis transported in 1828 for 14 years to New South Wales for stealing turkeys at Helmingham the year before |
| July 29th IJ | 1820 | Daniel | Clutterham | | Culpho | Burglary | reprieved |
| July 29th IJ | 1820 | Jehu | Collins | | Thornham & Thrandeston | Sheep stealing | reprieved |
| July 29th IJ | 1820 | Daniel | Rayner | | Mellis | Burglary | reprieved |
| Apr 7th SC | 1821 | Thomas | Mayes | 22 | Hadleigh | Theft | reprieved and transported for life to New South Wales in 1821 |
| Apr 7th SC | 1821 | Thomas | Josselyn | 20 | Hadleigh | Theft | reprieved and transported for life to New South Wales in 1821 |
| Apr 7th SC | 1821 | John | Lovett | 29 | Redlingfield | Stealing £5 | reprieved and transported for life to New South Wales in 1821 |
| Apr 7th SC | 1821 | Samuel | Grimwood | 38 | Easton | Burglary | Hanged – Ipswich April 28th Details SC April 14th |
| Apr 7th SC | 1821 | Thomas | Last | 38 | Easton | Burglary | respited and transported to Van Diemen's Land in 1821 |

| Date of trial report | Year | Christian name | Surname | Age | Place offence committed | Crime | Outcome |
|---|---|---|---|---|---|---|---|
| Apr 7th SC | 1821 | James | Rozier | 30 | Easton | Burglary | respited and transported to Van Diemen's Land in 1821 |
| Apr 7th SC | 1821 | John | Butcher | 47 | Oulton | Sheep stealing | respited and transported to Van Diemen's Land in 1821 |
| Apr 7th SC | 1821 | Robert | Randall | 19 | Bacton | Stealing £7 | reprieved |
| Apr 7th SC | 1821 | John | Freeman | 26 | Playford | Burglary in 1819 (having escaped from prison) | reprieved and transported for life to New South Wales in 1821 |
| Apr 7th SC | 1821 | Thomas | Craske | 26 | Beyton | Stealing a mare | reprieved and transported for life to New South Wales in 1821 |
| Apr 7th SC | 1821 | Jeremiah | Firman | 18 | Hengrave | Breaking & entering | reprieved and transported for life to New South Wales in 1821 |
| Apr 7th SC | 1821 | Henry | Gilly | 63 | Cowlinge | Stealing a lamb | reprieved |
| Apr 7th SC | 1821 | James | Weavers | 34 | Sudbury | Breaking & entering | reprieved SC April 21st and transported for life to New South Wales in 1821 |
| Apr 7th SC | 1821 | William | Downs | 36 | Sudbury | Breaking & entering | reprieved SC April 21st and transported for life to New South Wales in 1821 |
| Apr 7th SC | 1821 | John | Orams | 25 | Hargrave | Burglary | reprieved and transported for life to New South Wales in 1821 |
| Apr 7th SC | 1821 | William | Carlow | 20 | Hargrave | Burglary | reprieved SC April 21st and transported for life to New South Wales in 1821 |
| Apr 7th SC | 1821 | Timothy | Day | | Waldingfield | Sheep stealing | reprieved and transported for life to New South Wales in 1821 |
| Aug 11th IJ | 1821 | William | Farthing | 45 | Somersham | Sheep stealing | reprieved and transported for life to Van Diemen's Land in 1821 |
| Aug 11th IJ | 1821 | William | Gibbons | | Helmingham | Breaking & entering | reprieved |
| Aug 11th IJ | 1821 | Henry | Flack | 21 | Lakenheath | Burglary | reprieved - had previously been capitally convicted in 1819 |

| Date of trial report | Year | Christian name | Surname | Age | Place offence committed | Crime | Outcome |
|---|---|---|---|---|---|---|---|
| Apr 6th IJ | 1822 | William | Aldous | 17 | Stradbroke | Arson | Hanged - Ipswich April 20th 'at the drop over the Turnkey's Lodge' Details: IJ April 6th & 27th |
| Apr 6th IJ | 1822 | William | Ashman | 44 | Ickworth | Attacked gamekeeper | reprieved |
| Apr 6th IJ | 1822 | Richard | Bonnet | 42 | Ickworth | Assisted attack on gamekeeper | reprieved |
| Apr 6th IJ | 1822 | Thomas | Perry | 25 | Ickworth | Assisted attack on gamekeeper | reprieved |
| Apr 6th IJ | 1822 | John | Cook | 30 | Ickworth | Assisted attack on gamekeeper | reprieved |
| Apr 6th IJ | 1822 | Robert | Woollard | 26 | Ickworth | Assisted attack on gamekeeper | reprieved |
| Apr 6th IJ | 1822 | Robert | Underwood | 20 | Ickworth | Assisted attack on gamekeeper | reprieved |
| Apr 6th IJ | 1822 | William | Newman | | Gazeley | Sheep stealing | reprieved |
| Apr 6th IJ | 1822 | Lewis | Boswell | | Great Livermere | Burglary | reprieved - (gipsy) Details: IJ April 6th Transported for life to New South Wales in 1822 |
| Apr 6th IJ | 1822 | Ferdinand | Smith | | Great Livermere | Burglary | reprieved - (gipsy) Details: IJ April 6th |
| Apr 6th IJ | 1822 | Thomas | Tunmore | 59 | Watton, Norfolk | Stealing a mare | reprieved |
| Apr 6th IJ | 1822 | William | Snowling | 24 | Fressingfield | Burglary | reprieved and transported to New South Wales in 1822 |
| Apr 6th IJ | 1822 | William | Dow | 23 | Fressingfield | Burglary | reprieved and transported to Van Diemen's Land in 1822 |
| Apr 6th IJ | 1822 | Jacob | Taylor | 19 | Stowmarket | Burglary | reprieved and transported to Van Diemen's Land in 1822 |

| Date of trial report | Year | Christian name | Surname | Age | Place offence committed | Crime | Outcome |
|---|---|---|---|---|---|---|---|
| Aug 3rd SC | 1822 | **Robert** | **Bennett** | 48 | Mellis | Arson | **Hanged - Ipswich August 17th** Trial reported SC August 3rd, Execution reported SC August 25th |
| Aug 3rd SC | 1822 | **James** | **Phillips** | 40 | Hadleigh | Burglary | **Hanged - Bury St. Edmunds August 14th** Details: IJ August 17th |
| Aug 3rd SC | 1822 | **John** | **Wade** | 35 (or 44) | Hadleigh | Burglary | **Hanged - Bury St. Edmunds August 14th** Details: IJ August 17th |
| Aug 3rd SC | 1822 | Richard | Kemball | 23 | Hadleigh | Burglary | reprieved and transported for life to Van Diemen's Land in 1823 |
| Aug 3rd SC | 1822 | James | Wright | 24 | Hadleigh | Burglary | reprieved and transported for life to Van Diemen's Land in 1823 |
| Aug 3rd SC | 1822 | William | Thompson | 23 | Stuston | Burglary | reprieved and transported for life to New South Wales in 1823 |
| Aug 3rd SC | 1822 | William | Smith | 31 | Stuston | Burglary | reprieved and transported for life to Van Diemen's Land in 1823 |
| Aug 3rd SC | 1822 | Charles | Matthews | 23 | Beccles | Sheep stealing | reprieved |
| Apr 5th SC | 1823 | David | Bugg | 26 | Layham | Burglary | reprieved and transported for life to New South Wales in 1823 |
| Apr 5th SC | 1823 | Abraham | Bacon | 26 | Layham | Burglary | reprieved and transported for life to New South Wales in 1823 |
| Apr 5th SC | 1823 | Joseph | Ratcliffe | 22 | Layham | Burglary | reprieved and transported for life to New South Wales in 1823 |
| Apr 5th SC | 1823 | Abraham | Beeton | 24 | Exning | Sheep stealing | reprieved and transported for life to New South Wales in 1823 |
| Apr 5th SC | 1823 | James | Stebbings | 20 | Exning | Sheep stealing | reprieved and transported for life to Van Diemen's Land in 1824 |
| Apr 5th SC | 1823 | Allen | Crossman | 32 | Nether Hall, Bures | Breaking & entering | reprieved and transported for life to New South Wales in 1823 |
| Apr 5th SC | 1823 | John | Abbott | 30 | Stoke by Nayland | Sheep stealing | reprieved and transported for life to New South Wales in 1823 |

| Date of trial report | Year | Christian name | Surname | Age | Place offence committed | Crime | Outcome |
|---|---|---|---|---|---|---|---|
| Apr 5th SC | 1823 | Joshua | Johnson | 20 | Sproughton | Stealing a cow | reprieved and transported for life to New South Wales in 1823 |
| Apr 5th SC | 1823 | Isaac | Eaton | 21 | Bardwell | Stealing a pony | reprieved and transported for life to New South Wales in 1823 *(See Isaac Marrington, tried in 1819)* |
| Apr 5th SC | 1823 | Edward | Hasleton | 31 | Belstead | Sheep stealing | reprieved and transported for life to New South Wales in 1824 |
| Apr 5th SC | 1823 | Moses | Long | 20 | Brockford | Burglary | reprieved    Details:  SC April 5th Transported for life to New South Wales in 1828 for a theft in Wickham Skeith in 1827 |
| Apr 5th SC | 1823 | Gabriel | Nichol(a)s | 37 | Cavenham | Poaching with violence | reprieved and transported for life to New South Wales in 1823 |
| Apr 5th SC | 1823 | Thomas | Leonard | 36 | Cavenham | Poaching with violence | reprieved and transported for life to New South Wales in 1823 |
| Apr 5th SC | 1823 | Thomas | Christmas | 21 | Cavenham | Poaching with violence | reprieved and transported for life to New South Wales in 1823 |
| Apr 5th SC | 1823 | Samuel | Marlton | 21 | Cavenham | Poaching with violence | reprieved and transported for life to New South Wales in 1823 |
| July 26th/ Aug 2nd SC | 1823 | Abraham | Gill | 60 | Eriswell | Stealing a mare | reprieved |
| July 26th/ Aug 2nd SC | 1823 | John | Reeve | 21 | Eriswell | Stealing a mare | reprieved and transported for life to New South Wales in 1824 |
| July 26th/ Aug 2nd SC | 1823 | James | Cobbin(g) | 18 (or 28) | | Rape of a girl under 10 | reprieved and transported for life to New South Wales in 1824 |
| July 26th/ Aug 2nd SC | 1823 | Thomas | Taylor | 40 | Combs | Arson | reprieved after a plea for mercy, and transported for life to New South Wales in 1824 after being found guilty of stealing wood at Combs |

| Date of trial report | Year | Christian name | Surname | Age | Place offence committed | Crime | Outcome |
|---|---|---|---|---|---|---|---|
| July 26th/ Aug 2nd SC | 1823 | Robert | Wade | 20 | Tattingstone | Arson | Respited three times (SC August 16th & August 23rd) - transported for life to New South Wales in 1824 |
| Apr 3rd IJ | 1824 | **John** | **Chenery (or Cheney)** | 23 | Beccles | Burglary | **Hanged - Bury St. Edmunds April 21st** (Details IJ & SC April 10th; SC April 24th; BP April 21st) having confessed to a string of other offences |
| Apr 3rd IJ | 1824 | **Benjamin** | **Howlett** | 24 | Moulton | Burglary with violence | **Hanged - Bury St. Edmunds April 21st** (Details IJ & SC April 10th; SC April 24th; BP April 21st) having confessed to a string of other offences |
| Apr 3rd IJ | 1824 | **Thomas** | **Wright** | 26 | Glemsford | Burglary & pig stealing | **Hanged - Bury St. Edmunds April 21st** (Details IJ & SC April 10th; SC April 24th; BP April 21st) having confessed to a string of other offences |
| Apr 3rd IJ | 1824 | **Robert** | **Bradman (or Bradnam)** | 26 | Glemsford | Burglary & pig stealing | **Hanged - Bury St. Edmunds April 21st** (Details IJ & SC April 10th; SC April 24th; BP April 21st) having confessed to a string of other offences |
| Apr 3rd IJ | 1824 | Samuel | Bush | 20 | Stradbroke | Sheep stealing | reprieved, but transported for 14 years to Van Diemen's Land 20 years later for stealing one oaken plank. |
| Apr 3rd IJ | 1824 | William | Sparham | | Occold | Stealing clothes | reprieved |
| Apr 3rd IJ | 1824 | Thomas | Fenn | | Occold | Stealing clothes | reprieved |
| Apr 3rd IJ | 1824 | Edward | Bird | 17 | Blundeston | Burglary | reprieved |
| Apr 3rd IJ | 1824 | John | Philpot | 19 | Blundeston | Burglary | reprieved |
| Apr 3rd IJ | 1824 | Thomas | King | | Sproughton | Sheep stealing | reprieved |
| Apr 3rd IJ | 1824 | William | Beales | | Sproughton | Sheep stealing | reprieved |
| Apr 3rd IJ | 1824 | Henry | Loan (or Loawage) | 19 | Mendham | Theft from poor house | reprieved |

| Date of trial report | Year | Christian name | Surname | Age | Place offence committed | Crime | Outcome |
|---|---|---|---|---|---|---|---|
| Apr 3rd IJ | 1824 | William | Chipperfield | 19 | Lowestoft | Theft from poor house | reprieved and transported for life to New South Wales in 1825 |
| Apr 3rd IJ | 1824 | Henry | Botson | 19 | Lowestoft | Burglary | reprieved |
| Apr 3rd IJ | 1824 | Joseph | Carter | | Stowmarket | Burglary | reprieved and transported for life to New South Wales in 1824 |
| Apr 3rd IJ | 1824 | David | Southgate | | Stowmarket | Burglary | reprieved and transported for life to New South Wales in 1824 |
| Apr 3rd IJ | 1824 | William | Laughley (or Langley) | | Wrentham | Burglary | reprieved and transported for life to New South Wales in 1824 |
| Apr 3rd IJ | 1824 | William | Cranfield | 16 | Glemsford | Stealing a pig | spared on account of his youth and transported for life to New South Wales in 1824 |
| Apr 3rd IJ | 1824 | John | Levett | | Moulton | Burglary with violence | reprieved |
| Apr 3rd IJ | 1824 | Robert | Hensby | | Moulton | Burglary with violence | reprieved and transported for life to New South Wales in 1824 |
| Apr 3rd IJ | 1824 | Reuben | Bacon | 19 | Stoke | Sheep stealing | reprieved |
| Apr 3rd IJ | 1824 | Richard | Melton | | Stanstead | Burglary | reprieved and transported for life to New South Wales in 1824 |
| Apr 3rd IJ | 1824 | William | Saunders | | Stanstead | Burglary | reprieved and transported for life to New South Wales in 1824 |
| Apr 3rd IJ | 1824 | William | Whybrew (or Whybread) | | Cavendish | Burglary | reprieved and transported for life to New South Wales in 1824 |
| Apr 3rd IJ | 1824 | James | Brown | | Cavendish | Burglary | reprieved and transported for life to New South Wales in 1824 |
| Apr 3rd IJ | 1824 | James | Garnham | | Rickinghall | Sheep stealing | reprieved and transported for life to New South Wales in 1824 |
| Apr 3rd IJ | 1824 | James | Mansfield | | Glemsford | Burglary | reprieved |
| Apr 3rd IJ | 1824 | Thomas | Jeffes | | Great Dunmow | Stealing a pony | reprieved and transported for life to New South Wales in 1824 |

| Date of trial report | Year | Christian name | Surname | Age | Place offence committed | Crime | Outcome |
|---|---|---|---|---|---|---|---|
| Aug 14th IJ | 1824 | Edward | Sharpe | | Icklingham | Sheep stealing | reprieved and transported for life to New South Wales in 1824 |
| Aug 14th IJ | 1824 | John | Chinery | | Drinkstone | Breaking & entering | reprieved |
| Aug 14th IJ | 1824 | John | Wanham | | Drinkstone | Breaking & entering | reprieved and transported for life to New South Wales in 1824 |
| Aug 14th IJ | 1824 | Lovet James | Howard | | Drinkstone | Breaking & entering | reprieved and transported for life to New South Wales in 1824 |
| Aug 14th IJ | 1824 | William | Nicholls | | Mildenhall | Burglary | reprieved and transported for life to New South Wales in 1824 |
| Aug 14th IJ | 1824 | Samuel | Welton | | Kessingland | Sheep stealing | reprieved |
| Aug 14th IJ | 1824 | James | Woodgate | | Wenhaston | Stealing a mare | reprieved and transported for 14 years to New South Wales in 1825 |
| Aug 14th IJ | 1824 | George | Woodgate | | Hinton | Stealing clover seed | reprieved and transported for 14 years to New South Wales in 1825 |
| Aug 14th IJ | 1824 | Stephen | Baldry | | Hinton | Stealing clover seed | reprieved and transported for 14 years to New South Wales in 1825 |
| Aug 14th IJ | 1824 | Thomas | Barnaby | | Hinton | Stealing clover seed | reprieved and transported for life to New South Wales in 1825 |
| Aug 14th IJ | 1824 | Benjamin | Hazeltop (or Hazelip) | | Hinton | Stealing clover seed | reprieved and transported for life to New South Wales in 1825 |
| Aug 14th IJ | 1824 | Israel | Woodgate | | Hinton | Stealing clover seed | reprieved and transported for 14 years to New South Wales in 1825 |
| Mar 26 IJ | 1825 | Abraham | Summers (Somers) | | Bury | Burglary | reprieved and transported for life to New South Wales in 1825 |
| Mar 26 IJ | 1825 | Charles | Whiting | | Bury | Burglary | reprieved |
| Mar 26 IJ | 1825 | Samuel | Porter | | Bury | Burglary | reprieved and transported for 7 years to New South Wales in 1825 |
| Apr 2nd IJ | 1825 | John | Battley | | Nowton | Burglary | reprieved and transported for 14 years to New South Wales in 1825 Details IJ April 2nd |

| Date of trial report | Year | Christian name | Surname | Age | Place offence committed | Crime | Outcome |
| --- | --- | --- | --- | --- | --- | --- | --- |
| Apr 2nd IJ | 1825 | Thomas | Battley | | Nowton | Burglary | reprieved and transported for 14 years to New South Wales in 1825 Details IJ April 2nd |
| Apr 2nd IJ | 1825 | Thomas | Filer (or Filey) | | Nowton | Burglary | reprieved and transported for 14 years to New South Wales in 1825 Details IJ April 2nd |
| Apr 2nd IJ | 1825 | James | Butcher | | Nowton | Burglary | reprieved Details IJ April 2nd |
| Apr 2nd IJ | 1825 | William | Hogg | | Nowton | Burglary | reprieved and transported for 14 years to New South Wales in 1825 Details IJ April 2nd |
| Apr 2nd IJ | 1825 | Joseph Hartley | Stammers | 29 | Glemsford | Stealing to the value of 40s | reprieved and transported for 14 years to New South Wales in 1825 |
| Apr 2nd IJ | 1825 | James | Boutell | 21 | Stoke | Stealing to the value of 40s | reprieved and transported for 14 years to New South Wales in 1825 |
| Apr 2nd IJ | 1825 | Mark | Wright | 36 | Yoxford | Burglary | reprieved and transported for 14 years to New South Wales in 1825 |
| Apr 2nd IJ | 1825 | Sarah | Barnes | 24 | Layham | Highway robbery | reprieved and transported for life to Van Diemen's Land in 1825 Details IJ April 2nd |
| Apr 2nd IJ | 1825 | Isaac | Foulsham | 20 | Reydon | Burglary | reprieved and transported for 14 years to New South Wales in 1825 |
| Apr 2nd IJ | 1825 | William | Middleton | 20 | Reydon | Burglary | reprieved and transported for 14 years to New South Wales in 1825 |
| Apr 2nd IJ | 1825 | John | Tasker | 28 | Great Waldingfield | Burglary | reprieved and transported for 14 years to New South Wales in 1825 Details SC April 2nd |
| Apr 2nd IJ | 1825 | Robert | Morris | 19 | Great Waldingfield | Burglary | reprieved and transported for 14 years to New South Wales in 1825 Details SC April 2nd |
| Apr 2nd IJ | 1825 | George | King | | Rushmere | Stealing money | reprieved |

| Date of trial report | Year | Christian name | Surname | Age | Place offence committed | Crime | Outcome |
|---|---|---|---|---|---|---|---|
| Apr 2nd IJ | 1825 | Sampson/ Samuel | Curtis | 27 | Wissett | Sheep stealing | reprieved - see conviction in August 1827) |
| Apr 2nd IJ | 1825 | Thomas | Parker | | Aldringham | Stealing wheat | reprieved |
| Apr 2nd IJ | 1825 | John | Parker | | Aldringham | Stealing wheat | reprieved; was probably the same John Parker who was transported for 7 years to Van Diemen's Land in 1833 for theft of barley at Kelsale in 1829 |
| Aug 6th SC | 1825 | **John** | **Mann** | 27 | Hadleigh | Highway robbery | **Hanged - Bury St. Edmunds August 20th** despite a respite until that date  Details SC August 6th |
| Aug 6th SC | 1825 | Thomas | Grimsey | 21 | Hadleigh | Highway robbery | reprieved and transported for life to New South Wales in 1825 Details SC August 6th |
| Apr 1st SC | 1826 | Robert | Mauldon (Malden) | | Melton | Burglary | reprieved |
| Apr 1st SC | 1826 | George | Jessup | 11 | Rickinghall | Stealing from a house | reprieved |
| Apr 1st SC | 1826 | Mark | Wix | 18 | Mendlesham | Stealing from a house | reprieved and transported for life to Van Diemen's Land in 1826 |
| Apr 1st SC | 1826 | James | Norman | | Cornard | Burglary | reprieved |
| Apr 1st SC | 1826 | Isaac | Jeffery | | Cornard | Burglary | reprieved and sentenced to transportation, but pardoned.  Convicted in 1831 and transported for 7 years to New South Wales in 1832 for theft of an ass at Little Cornard |
| Apr 1st SC | 1826 | Stephen | Fish | | Groton | Stealing a cow | reprieved and transported for life to Van Diemen's Land in 1826 |
| Apr 1st SC | 1826 | John (or Jonathan) | Stribling | | Lavenham | Sheep stealing | reprieved and transported for life to Van Diemen's Land in 1826 |
| Apr 1st SC | 1826 | William | Ware | 20 | Harrow | Horse stealing | reprieved and transported for life to Van Diemen's Land in 1826 |

| Date of trial report | Year | Christian name | Surname | Age | Place offence committed | Crime | Outcome |
|---|---|---|---|---|---|---|---|
| Apr 1st SC | 1826 | Robert | Fox | 20 | Harrow | Horse stealing | reprieved and transported for life to Van Diemen's Land in 1826 |
| July 22nd SC | 1826 | Robert | Rule | | Alpheton | Highway robbery | reprieved and transported for life to Van Diemen's Land in 1827 |
| July 22nd SC | 1826 | Edward | Green | 21 | Melton | Breaking & entering | reprieved and transported for life to New South Wales in 1826 |
| July 22nd SC | 1826 | Thomas | Smith | | Sudbury | Stealing a pony | reprieved and transported for life to Van Diemen's Land in 1827 |
| July 22nd SC | 1826 | John | Clark | | Glemsford | Burglary | reprieved and transported for life to Van Diemen's Land in 1827 |
| July 22nd SC | 1826 | John | Spalding | | Fressingfield | Breaking & entering | reprieved and transported for life to Van Diemen's Land in 1827 |
| July 22nd SC | 1826 | Elizabeth | Hulstone (Hailstone) | | Thurston | Stealing from her master | reprieved and transported for life to Van Diemen's Land in 1826 |
| Apr 7th IJ | 1827 | Thomas | Boss | 21 | Bassingham, Lincs | Stealing a colt | Sentence of death - reprieved and transported to Van Diemen's Land in 1827 |
| Apr 7th IJ | 1827 | Moses | Boss | 19 | Bassingham, Lincs | Stealing a colt | Sentence of death - reprieved and transported to Van Diemen's Land in 1827 |
| Apr 7th IJ | 1827 | William | Cable | | Capel St. Andrew & Yaxley | Stealing a mare & stealing trousers | Death recorded & sentenced to be transported for life though there is no trace of him going |
| Apr 7th IJ | 1827 | William | Arnold | | Wherstead | Sheep stealing | Death recorded   Details SC April 7th reprieved and transported for life to Van Diemen's Land in 1827 |
| Apr 7th IJ | 1827 | Robert | Halls | | Wherstead | Sheep stealing | Death recorded   Details SC April 7th reprieved and transported for life to Van Diemen's Land in 1827 |
| Apr 7th IJ | 1827 | Henry | Cooper | | Hollesley | Stealing a lamb | Death recorded   Details SC April 7th |

| Date of trial report | Year | Christian name | Surname | Age | Place offence committed | Crime | Outcome |
| --- | --- | --- | --- | --- | --- | --- | --- |
| Apr 7th IJ | 1827 | John | Smith alias Saunders | | Lilley, Herts | Horse stealing | Sentence of death - reprieved and transported to Van Diemen's Land in 1827 |
| Apr 7th IJ | 1827 | William | Smith alias Saunders | | Lilley, Herts | Horse stealing | Sentence of death - reprieved and transported to Van Diemen's Land in 1827 |
| Apr 7th IJ | 1827 | William | Pale | | Lilley, Herts | Horse stealing | Sentence of death - reprieved and transported to Van Diemen's Land in 1827 |
| Apr 7th IJ | 1827 | James | Smith | | Felsham | Stealing fabrics | Death recorded |
| Aug 4th IJ | 1827 | Sampson | Curtis | | Linstead | Burglary | Death recorded - had received a capital conviction in 1825 for sheep stealing at Wissett  Transported for life to New South Wales in 1828 |
| Aug 4th IJ | 1827 | Samuel | Clow | | Clopton | Burglary | Death recorded - having been recaptured after breaking out of Ipswich gaol  Transported for life to New South Wales in 1828 |
| Aug 11th IJ | 1827 | James | King | | Boxford | Sheep stealing | Death recorded |
| Aug 11th IJ | 1827 | William | Pollard | | Lakenham, Nfk. | Stealing a pony | Death recorded, but reprieved and transported for life to Van Diemen's Land in 1828 |
| Aug 11th IJ | 1827 | John | Hampstead alias Farrant | | Stoke by Clare | Stealing a gelding | Death recorded, but reprieved and transported for life to Van Diemen's Land in 1828 |
| Aug 11th IJ | 1827 | John | Burleigh | | St. James Southelmham | Stealing leather | Death recorded, but reprieved and transported for life to Van Diemen's Land in 1827 |

| Date of trial report | Year | Christian name | Surname | Age | Place offence committed | Crime | Outcome |
|---|---|---|---|---|---|---|---|
| Aug 11th IJ | 1827 | Moses | Long | | Wickham Skeith | Burglary | Death recorded, but reprieved and transported for life to New South Wales in 1828 |
| Aug 11th IJ | 1827 | Edward | Threagle | | Occold | Burglary | Death recorded |
| Aug 11th IJ | 1827 | William | Baxter | | Tunstall | Stealing money | Death recorded, but reprieved and transported for 14 years to New South Wales in 1828 |
| Aug 11th IJ | 1827 | James | Cook Jnr. | | Yoxford | Stealing 60 sovereigns | Death recorded, but reprieved and transported for life to New South Wales in 1828 |
| Mar 29th IJ | 1828 | James | Peachey | 27 | Wetherden (He came from Bacton) | Burglary with violence | Sentence of death - reprieved April 5th (IJ) Details SC March 29th Transported for life to New South Wales in 1828 |
| Mar 29th IJ | 1828 | William | Alexander | 26 | Wetherden (He came from Bacton) | Burglary with violence | Sentence of death - reprieved April 5th (IJ) Details SC March 29th Transported for life to New South Wales in 1828 |
| Mar 29th IJ | 1828 | George | Leabon | 22 | Yaxley (He came from Bacton) | Breaking & entering | Sentence of death - reprieved April 5th (IJ) Details SC March 29th Transported for life to New South Wales in 1828 |
| Mar 29th IJ | 1828 | Henry | Smith alias Nunn | 17 | Washbrook & Bentley | Stealing a horse & saddle | Death recorded but reprieved and transported for life to New South Wales in 1828 |
| Mar 29th IJ | 1828 | Robert | Abbott | 16 | Wetheringsett | Burglary | Death recorded but reprieved and transported for life to New South Wales in 1828 |
| Mar 29th IJ | 1828 | Samuel | Rose | 18 | Wetheringsett | Burglary | Death recorded but reprieved and transported for life to New South Wales in 1828 |

| Date of trial report | Year | Christian name | Surname | Age | Place offence committed | Crime | Outcome |
|---|---|---|---|---|---|---|---|
| Mar 29th IJ | 1828 | William | King | 25 | Woodbridge | Stealing fabrics | Death recorded  Details SC March 29th |
| Mar 29th IJ | 1828 | Edward | Kitson | 27 | Woodbridge | Stealing fabrics | Death recorded  Details SC March 29th Transported for life to New South Wales in 1828 |
| Mar 29th IJ | 1828 | John | Day | 26 | Yoxford | Stealing meat | Death recorded  Details SC March 29th Transported for life to New South Wales in 1828 |
| Mar 29th IJ | 1828 | William | Shave | 17 | Thornham | Burglary | Death recorded |
| Mar 29th IJ | 1828 | John | Paxman | 60 | Bungay | Stealing pewter | Death recorded |
| Mar 29th IJ | 1828 | John | Crowder | 26 | Beccles | Burglary | Death recorded  Details SC March 29th Transported for life to Van Diemen's Land in 1829 |
| Mar 29th IJ | 1828 | Edward | Canham | 32 | Screveton, Notts | Horse stealing | Death recorded but reprieved and transported for life to New South Wales in 1828 |
| Apr 5th IJ | 1828 | Charles | Jones (IJ) or White (SC) | 19 | Sudbury | Breaking & entering | Death recorded but reprieved and transported for life to New South Wales in 1828 |
| Apr 5th IJ | 1828 | Thomas | Bantock | 36 | Hawstead | Stealing a heifer | Death recorded - probably the same Thomas Bantock capitally convicted for stealing a cow at Badwell Ash in 1820  Transported for life to New South Wales in 1828 |
| Apr 5th SC | 1828 | James | Oakley | 25 | Glemsford | Horse stealing | Death recorded but reprieved and transported for life to New South Wales in 1828 |
| Apr 5th SC | 1828 | John | Humm | 24 | Glemsford | Horse stealing | Death recorded but reprieved and transported for life to New South Wales in 1828 |

| Date of trial report | Year | Christian name | Surname | Age | Place offence committed | Crime | Outcome |
|---|---|---|---|---|---|---|---|
| Aug 9th IJ | 1828 | Lionel | Lee | | Tannington | Robbing his master | Death recorded   Details IJ & SC   August 9th   Transported for life to Van Diemen's Land in 1829 |
| Aug 9th IJ | 1828 | **William** | **Corder** | 24 | Polstead | Murder | **Hanged - Bury St. Edmunds August 12th**   Details SC August 9th & 15th include trial, confession, hanging and dissection of the body in much detail |
| Aug 9th IJ | 1828 | Joseph | Bullen | 19 | Metfield | Breaking & entering | Death recorded - probably the same Joseph Bullen capitally convicted for stealing a watch in 1817   Details IJ & SC   August 9th   Transported for life to Van Diemen's Land in 1829   His son of the same name followed him in 1842 |
| Aug 9th IJ | 1828 | Osborne | Bush | | Metfield | Breaking & entering | Death recorded   Details IJ & SC   August 9th   Transported for life to Van Diemen's Land in 1829 |
| Aug 9th IJ | 1828 | Henry | Frazer | | Worlington | Stealing a watch | Death recorded |
| Aug 9th IJ | 1828 | William | Dean | 18 | Gipping | Stealing a watch | Death recorded, but reprieved and transported for life to Van Diemen's Land in 1829 |
| Aug 9th IJ | 1828 | Charles | Bruce | | Hadleigh | Burglary | Death recorded but reprieved and transported for life to New South Wales in 1828 |
| Apr 11th SC | 1829 | **William** | **Cattermole** | 18 | Letheringham | Arson | **Hanged - Ipswich April 25th**   Details of case: SC April 11th. (Judge & court surprised at guilty verdict)   Details of execution: SC May 2nd |
| Apr 11th SC | 1829 | **George** | **Partridge** | 23 | Milden near Monks Eleigh | Murder | **Hanged - Bury St. Edmunds April 13th**   Details of case: SC April 11th   Details of execution: SC April 18th |

| Date of trial report | Year | Christian name | Surname | Age | Place offence committed | Crime | Outcome |
|---|---|---|---|---|---|---|---|
| Apr 11th SC | 1829 | **Thomas** | **Hubbard** | 20 | Mendham | Housebreaking | **Hanged - Ipswich April 25th** Details of case: SC April 11th. Details of execution: SC May 2nd |
| Apr 11th SC | 1829 | John | Knights | | Bungay | Burglary | Death recorded, but reprieved and transported for 7 years to Van Diemen's Land in 1829 |
| Apr 11th SC | 1829 | John | Thurlow | | Saxmundham | Stealing a pony gig | Death recorded, but reprieved and transported for 7 years to Van Diemen's Land in 1829 |
| Apr 11th SC | 1829 | George | Burrows | | Alderton | Sheep stealing | Death recorded  Details: SC April 11th |
| Apr 11th SC | 1829 | Henry | Stollery | | Alderton | Sheep stealing | Death recorded  Details: SC April 11th |
| Apr 11th SC | 1829 | David | Stollery | | Alderton | Sheep stealing | Death recorded  Details: SC April 11th |
| Apr 11th SC | 1829 | Collins | Edwards | | Darsham | Stealing a gelding | Death recorded, but reprieved and transported for 7 years to Van Diemen's Land in 1829 |
| Apr 11th SC | 1829 | David | Barkom (or Barham) | | Sweffling | Housebreaking | Death recorded, but reprieved and transported for 7 years to Van Diemen's Land in 1829 |
| Apr 11th SC | 1829 | William | Matthews | | Foxhall | Burglary (whilst the family were at church) | Death recorded, but reprieved and transported for 7 years to Van Diemen's Land in 1829 |
| Apr 11th SC | 1829 | Joseph | Read | | Carlton Colville | Burglary (whilst the family were at church) | Death recorded, but reprieved and transported for 7 years to Van Diemen's Land in 1829 |
| Apr 11th SC | 1829 | John | Loveday | | Barton Mills | Stealing a mare | Death recorded, but reprieved and transported for life to New South Wales in 1830 |
| Apr 18th SC | 1829 | John | Hammond | | Bury St. Edmunds | Fraudulently obtaining money | Death recorded  Details: SC April 18th Reprieved and transported for life to New South Wales in 1830 |

| Date of trial report | Year | Christian name | Surname | Age | Place offence committed | Crime | Outcome |
|---|---|---|---|---|---|---|---|
| Aug 8th SC | 1829 | Leabon | Lee | | Ringshall | Burglary | Death recorded, but reprieved and transported for life to New South Wales in 1830 |
| Aug 8th SC | 1829 | John | Barker | | Ringshall | Burglary | Death recorded, but reprieved and transported for life to New South Wales in 1830 |
| Aug 8th SC | 1829 | Robert | Woods | | Saxmundham | Forgery | Death recorded |
| Aug 8th SC | 1829 | Edward Benjamin | Bird | | Parham | Burglary | Death recorded |
| Aug 8th SC | 1829 | Mary Ann | Freeman | 18 | Parham | Burglary | Death recorded, but reprieved and transported for 7 years to Van Diemen's Land in 1829 |
| Aug 15th SC | 1829 | Thomas | Wright | 20 | Edwardstone | Robbery | Death recorded  Details: SC August 15th  Reprieved and transported for life to New South Wales in 1830 |
| Aug 15th SC | 1829 | Benjamin | Whymark | 18 | Edwardstone | Robbery | Death recorded  Details: SC August 15th  Reprieved and transported for life to Van Diemen's Land in 1830 |
| Aug 15th SC | 1829 | William | Viall | 16 | Clare | Cutting & maiming with intent to murder | Sentence of death. Details: SC August 15th. Report of respite SC August 22nd  Reprieved and transported for life, on account of his youth, to New South Wales in 1830 |
| Aug 15th SC | 1829 | Henry | Perring | 18 | Cavendish | Housebreaking | Death recorded, but reprieved and transported for life to New South Wales in 1830 |
| Aug 15th SC | 1829 | Thomas | Sparks | 20 | Wixoe | Burglary (whilst the family were at church) | Death recorded, but reprieved and transported for life to New South Wales in 1830 |

| Date of trial report | Year | Christian name | Surname | Age | Place offence committed | Crime | Outcome |
|---|---|---|---|---|---|---|---|
| Aug 15th SC | 1829 | Samuel | Calver alias Peck | 20 | Ashfield | Stealing a gelding | Death recorded, but reprieved and transported for life to Van Diemen's Land in 1830 |
| Apr 3rd SC | 1830 | James | Clarke | 24 | Palgrave | Stealing 7 oxen | Death recorded  Details: SC April 3rd Reprieved and transported for life to New South Wales in 1830 |
| Apr 3rd SC | 1830 | **Samuel** | **Wright** | 33 | Claydon | Unnatural crime (sodomy of a boy of 9) | **Hanged - Ipswich April 17th** Details of case: SC April 3rd |
| Apr 3rd SC | 1830 | Francis | Botright | 25 | Great Yarmouth | Assault & theft | Death recorded  Details: SC April 3rd |
| Apr 3rd SC | 1830 | Mary | Mitchell | 19 | Kirtley | Stealing money | Death recorded  Details: SC April 3rd |
| Apr 3rd SC | 1830 | Abel | Garrod | 23 | Blythford | Breaking & entering | Death recorded  Details: SC April 3rd Reprieved and transported for life to New South Wales in 1830 |
| Apr 3rd SC | 1830 | William | Cullingford | 21 | Blythford | Breaking & entering | Death recorded  Details: SC April 3rd Reprieved and transported for life to New South Wales in 1830 |
| Apr 3rd SC | 1830 | Manister | Worts | 21 | Sudbury | Housebreaking from vicar's house on Sunday | Death recorded |
| Apr 3rd SC | 1830 | Ephraim | Leggatt | 21 | Rougham | Housebreaking | Death recorded, but reprieved and transported for life to New South Wales in 1830 |
| Apr 3rd SC | 1830 | William | Paine | 22 | Ixworth | Stealing a ewe | Death recorded, but reprieved and transported for 7 years to New South Wales in 1830 |
| Apr 3rd SC | 1830 | Robert | Paine | 21 | Ixworth | Stealing a ewe | Death recorded, but reprieved and transported for 7 years to New South Wales in 1830 |

| Date of trial report | Year | Christian name | Surname | Age | Place offence committed | Crime | Outcome |
|---|---|---|---|---|---|---|---|
| Apr 3rd SC | 1830 | David | Mott | 33 | Cowlinge | Stealing a ewe | Death recorded, but reprieved and transported for 7 years to New South Wales in 1830 |
| Aug 7th SC | 1830 | John | Savage | | Rougham | Stealing a ewe | Death recorded, but reprieved and transported for 7 years to Van Diemen's Land in 1831 |
| Aug 7th SC | 1830 | William | Savage | | Rougham | Stealing a ewe | Death recorded, but reprieved and transported for 7 years to Van Diemen's Land in 1831 |
| Aug 7th SC | 1830 | Stephen | Balls | | Westleton | Breaking & entering | Death recorded   Had been acquitted at previous Assize for robbery at Blyford for which others were found guilty (turned King's evidence). Reprieved and transported for life to Van Diemen's Land in 1831. |
| Aug 7th SC | 1830 | Robert | Reynolds | | Westleton | Breaking & entering | Death recorded   Had been acquitted at previous Assize for robbery at Blyford for which others were found guilty.   Reprieved and transported for 7 years to Van Diemen's Land in 1831, but died on the voyage. |
| Aug 7th SC | 1830 | Robert | West | | Wortham | Sheep stealing | Death recorded |
| Aug 7th SC | 1830 | John | Potter | | Huntingfield | Stealing a bull calf | Death recorded |
| Aug 7th SC | 1830 | William | Hawes | | Hoxne | Stealing clothing | Death recorded |
| Aug 7th SC | 1830 | Edmund | Duffield | | Attleborough, Nfk. | Stealing a pony | Death recorded |
| Aug 7th SC | 1830 | John | Clark | | Bricet | Stealing a mare | Death recorded, but reprieved and transported for life to Van Diemen's Land in 1831 |

| Date of trial report | Year | Christian name | Surname | Age | Place offence committed | Crime | Outcome |
|---|---|---|---|---|---|---|---|
| Aug 7th SC | 1830 | Robert | Sage | | Bricet | Stealing a mare | Death recorded, but reprieved and transported for life to Van Diemen's Land in 1831 |
| Mar 26th SC | 1831 | Charles | Lovely | 21 | Needham Market | Burglary | Death recorded. Details: SC March 26th Transported for life to New South Wales in 1831 |
| Mar 26th SC | 1831 | George | Day | 18 | Needham Market | Burglary | Death recorded. Details: SC March 26th Sentenced to be transported for life but never sent. |
| Mar 26th SC | 1831 | James | Pinfold | 20 | Hemingstone | Robbery with violence | Death recorded. Details: SC March 26th Transported for life to Van Diemen's Land in 1831 |
| Mar 26th SC | 1831 | Richard | Bolton | 28 | Aldeburgh | Violent assault | Death recorded. Details: SC March 26th |
| Mar 26th SC | 1831 | William | Coppin | 18 | Wortham | Stealing from a house | Death recorded. Details: SC March 26th Transported for life to New South Wales in 1831 |
| Mar 26th SC | 1831 | Henry | King | 19 | Wortham | Stealing from a house | Death recorded. Details: SC March 26th Transported for life to New South Wales in 1831 |
| Mar 26th SC | 1831 | Henry | Brown | 19 | Wortham | Stealing from a house | Death recorded. Details: SC March 26th Transported for life to New South Wales in 1831 |
| Mar 26th SC | 1831 | John | Garnham | 18 | Wortham | Stealing from a house | Death recorded. Details: SC March 26th Transported for life to New South Wales in 1831. The second Garnham from the area in this list. |
| Mar 26th SC | 1831 | John | Smith | 29 | Long Melford | Breaking & entering | Death recorded Transported for 14 years to Van Diemen's Land in 1831. |

| Date of trial report | Year | Christian name | Surname | Age | Place offence committed | Crime | Outcome |
|---|---|---|---|---|---|---|---|
| Mar 26th SC | 1831 | James | Smith | 22 | Sudbury | Breaking & entering | Death recorded. Though he does not appear to have been transported this time, a number by this name were subsequently sent as convicts to Australia. |
| Mar 26th SC | 1831 | Thomas | Elliston | 18 | Sudbury | Breaking & entering | Death recorded |
| Mar 26th SC | 1831 | Edward | Mayes | 30 | Pakenham | Breaking & entering | Death recorded.  Probably the same Edward Mayes transported for 7 years to Van Diemen's Land in 1835 for a felony committed the year before. |
| Mar 26th SC | 1831 | William | Matthews | 19 | Pakenham | Burglary | Death recorded  Transported for 14 years to Van Diemen's Land in 1831. |
| Mar 26th SC | 1831 | William | Nunn | 21 | Pakenham | Burglary | Death recorded  Transported for 14 years to Van Diemen's Land in 1831. |
| Mar 26th SC | 1831 | Robert | Rogers | 22 | Pakenham | Burglary | Death recorded  Transported for 14 years to Van Diemen's Land in 1831. |
| Mar 26th SC | 1831 | Joseph | Speller | a boy | Bury St. Edmunds | Stealing silver | Death recorded |
| Mar 26th SC | 1831 | George | Jackson | a boy | Bury St. Edmunds | Stealing silver | Death recorded.  Transported for 7 years to New South Wales in 1833, presumably after 2 years in the Penitentiary. |
| Mar 26th SC | 1831 | Mark | Pitch | 51 (or 60) | Tuddenham | Stealing hops | Possibly death recorded, but commuted to 14 years transportation, reduced to 7 years. Details: SC March 26th.  Transported to Van Diemen's Land in 1831. |
| July 23rd SC | 1831 | Henry | Smith | 31 | Lavenham | Breaking & entering | Death recorded.  Transported for life to New South Wales in 1831. |
| July 23rd SC | 1831 | Charles | Codd | 22 | Buxhall | Sheep stealing | Death recorded.  Transported for life to New South Wales in 1831. |

| Date of trial report | Year | Christian name | Surname | Age | Place offence committed | Crime | Outcome |
|---|---|---|---|---|---|---|---|
| July 23rd SC | 1831 | James | Burrows | 15 | Grundisburgh | Breaking & entering | Death recorded. Transported for life to New South Wales in 1831. |
| July 23rd SC | 1831 | George | Gardiner | 21 | Newton, Sudbury | Violent robbery | Death recorded. Transported for life to New South Wales in 1832. |
| July 23rd SC | 1831 | Sarah | Collins | 18 | Newton, Sudbury | Violent robbery | Death recorded. Transported for life to New South Wales in 1831. |
| July 23rd SC | 1831 | Henry | Munns | 16 | Exning | Sheep stealing | Death recorded. Transported for life to New South Wales in 1831. |
| July 23rd SC | 1831 | Edward | Munns | 30 | Exning | Sheep stealing | Death recorded |
| July 23rd SC | 1831 | James | Nunn | | Wattisfield | Burglary | Death recorded. Transported for life to New South Wales in 1831. |
| July 23rd SC | 1831 | Samuel | Addison | 21 | Botesdale | Stealing a gelding | Death recorded. Details: SC July 23rd |
| July 30th SC | 1831 | James | Butcher | 21 | Framlingham | Arson | Death recorded. Details: SC July 30th This trial had been postponed twice before; two others were found not guilty of the same offence. Transported for life to New South Wales in 1831. |
| July 30th SC | 1831 | Ambrose | Flack | 48 | Ipswich | Murder | Hanged - Ipswich July 25th. Details of case and execution SC July 30th 1831. |
| Mar 17th SC | 1832 | Thomas | Shalders | 66 | Sutton | Horse stealing | Death recorded. Details: SC March 17th Transported for life to Van Diemen's Land in 1832. |
| Mar 17th SC | 1832 | Stephen | Gilbert | 40 | Sutton | Horse stealing | Death recorded. Details: SC March 17th |
| Mar 17th SC | 1832 | Thomas | Staines | 20 | Glemsford | Burglary | Death recorded |
| Mar 17th SC | 1832 | Charles | Staines | 16 | Glemsford | Burglary | Death recorded. Transported for life to New South Wales in 1832. |
| Mar 24th SC | 1832 | Charles | Manning | 20 | Theberton | Breaking & entering | Death recorded |
| Mar 24th SC | 1832 | David | Kett | 15 | Theberton | Breaking & entering | Death recorded |

| Date of trial report | Year | Christian name | Surname | Age | Place offence committed | Crime | Outcome |
|---|---|---|---|---|---|---|---|
| Mar 24th SC | 1832 | John | Mayhew | 16 | Wenhaston | Breaking & entering | Death recorded - stole 5 loaves of bread |
| Mar 24th SC | 1832 | David | Robinson | 16 | Stradbroke | Breaking & entering | Death recorded - stole from his father's shop. Details: SC March 24th 1832. Transported for 7 years, increased to 14 years to Van Diemen's Land in 1832. |
| Mar 24th SC | 1832 | Robert | Howes | 20 | Stradbroke | Theft | Death recorded |
| Mar 24th SC | 1832 | Henry | Parr | 19 | Oulton | Sheep stealing | Death recorded  Transported for life to Van Diemen's Land in 1832. |
| Mar 24th SC | 1832 | William | Saunders | 18 | Halesworth | Stealing rabbit skins | Death recorded |
| Mar 24th SC | 1832 | Robert | Thwaites | 26 | Copdock | Burglary | Death recorded  Transported for life to Van Diemen's Land in 1832. |
| Mar 24th SC | 1832 | James | Wiskins | 38 | Wingfield | Sheep stealing | Death recorded  Transported for life to Van Diemen's Land in 1832. |
| Mar 24th SC | 1832 | Henry | Shepherd | 18 | Barningham | Stealing money | Death recorded.  Transported for 7 years to New South Wales in 1832. |
| Mar 24th SC | 1832 | John | Scowen | 30 | Boxford | Sheep stealing | Death recorded |
| Mar 24th SC | 1832 | Joseph | Coote | 41 | Bury St. Edmunds | Sheep stealing | Death recorded  Transported for life to Van Diemen's Land in 1832. |
| Mar 24th SC | 1832 | Charles | Ward | 25 | Bury St. Edmunds | Sheep stealing | Death recorded |
| Mar 24th SC | 1832 | James | Smith | 36 | Bury St. Edmunds | Sheep stealing | Death recorded  Transported for life to Van Diemen's Land in 1832. |
| Mar 24th SC | 1832 | Isaac | Coote | 17 | Sudbury | Burglary | Death recorded |
| Mar 24th SC | 1832 | William | Howell | 17 | Sudbury | Burglary | Death recorded.  Transported for life to New South Wales in 1832. |
| Mar 24th SC | 1832 | Robert | Bryant | 16 | Hadleigh | Sacrilege (stole from Hadleigh Church) | Death recorded.  Convicted on the evidence of an accomplice, George Rand, aged 12. Transported for life to New South Wales in 1832. |

| Date of trial report | Year | Christian name | Surname | Age | Place offence committed | Crime | Outcome |
|---|---|---|---|---|---|---|---|
| Mar 24th SC | 1832 | William | Baker | 17 | Hadleigh | Sacrilege (stole from Hadleigh Church) | Death recorded. Convicted on the evidence of an accomplice, George Rand, aged 12. Transported for life to New South Wales in 1832. |
| Mar 24th SC | 1832 | Simon | Frost | 20 | Nowton | Highway robbery | Sentence of death, respited following a petition from the inhabitants of Hessett where he lived. Details: IJ March 31st. Executed on the way to New South Wales for a murder committed on board. Details: IJ August 18th 1832 |
| Aug 4th SC | 1832 | **Benjamin** | **Edwards** | 27 | Westleton | Arson | **Sentence of death – Hanged Ipswich August 18th.** Details of trial: SC August 4th. |
| Aug 4th SC | 1832 | **James** | **Strowger/ Stroulger** | 26 (or 22) | Westleton | Arson | **Sentence of death – Hanged Ipswich August 18th.** Details of trial: SC August 4th |
| Aug 4th SC | 1832 | **William** | **Twitchett/ Turtchell** | 27 | Stradishall | Burglary with violence | **Sentence of death – Hanged Bury August 15th.** Details of trial: SC August 4th; details of execution, SC August 18th. |
| Aug 4th SC | 1832 | William | Gilly | 18 | Stradishall | Burglary with violence | Death recorded - guilty along with Twitchett; mercy shewn on account of his youth. Transported for 14 years to New South Wales in 1833. |
| Aug 4th SC | 1832 | John | Burgess | 19 | Badwell Ash | Burglary | Death recorded. Transported to Van Diemen's Land in 1832. |
| Aug 4th SC | 1832 | Ralph | Rayner | 18 | Fornham All Saints | Robbery with violence | Death recorded |
| Aug 4th SC | 1832 | William | Knott | 34 | Belton | Burglary | Death recorded. Transported for 14 years to New South Wales in 1833. |

| Date of trial report | Year | Christian name | Surname | Age | Place offence committed | Crime | Outcome |
|---|---|---|---|---|---|---|---|
| Aug 4th SC | 1832 | William | Bensley | 29 | Belton | Burglary | Death recorded. Transported for 14 years to Van Diemen's Land in 1832 |
| Mar 23rd SC | 1833 | Robert | List | 23 | Kenton | Stealing from a house | Death recorded Details: SC March 23rd |
| Mar 23rd SC | 1833 | Isaac | List | 19 | Kenton | Stealing from a house | Death recorded Details: SC March 23rd |
| Mar 23rd SC | 1833 | John | Bays | 20 | Hadleigh | Burglary | Death recorded Details: SC March 23rd. Transported for life to Van Diemen's Land in 1835 for stealing hens at Aldham the previous year. |
| Mar 23rd SC | 1833 | John | Smith | 35 | Ampton | Burglary | Death recorded Details: SC March 23rd - stole from Lord Calthorpe. Transported for 14 years to New South Wales in 1833. |
| Mar 23rd SC | 1833 | Francis | Botwright | 26 | Gorleston | Robbery with violence | Death recorded Details: SC March 23rd. Transported for life to New South Wales in 1834 |
| Mar 23rd SC | 1833 | Thomas | Smith | 22 | Gorleston | Robbery with violence | Death recorded Details: SC March 23rd |
| Mar 23rd SC | 1833 | Samuel | Tubby | 28 | Beccles | Burglary | Death recorded Details: SC March 23rd. Transported for life to New South Wales in 1834, following a trial that year for a further theft in Lowestoft.. |
| Mar 23rd SC | 1833 | Charles | Rose | 20 | Rickinghall | Burglary | Death recorded |
| Mar 23rd SC | 1833 | William | Palmer | | Haughley | Stealing clothing | Death recorded Details: SC March 23rd. Transported for life to New South Wales in 1833 |
| Mar 23rd SC | 1833 | Henry | Fitz James | | Haughley | Stealing clothing | Death recorded Details: SC March 23rd. Transported for life to New South Wales in 1833 |
| Mar 23rd SC | 1833 | Frederick | Imhoff (or Immock) | | Haughley | Stealing clothing | Death recorded Details: SC March 23rd. Transported for life to New South Wales in 1833 |

| Date of trial report | Year | Christian name | Surname | Age | Place offence committed | Crime | Outcome |
|---|---|---|---|---|---|---|---|
| Aug 3rd SC | 1833 | Thomas | Smith | 23 | Beyton | Burglary | Death recorded  Details SC August 3rd. Transported for 14 years to New South Wales in 1834. |
| Aug 3rd SC | 1833 | Samuel | Sprucett or Sprunt | 30 | Lowestoft | Stealing meat | Death recorded |
| Aug 3rd SC | 1833 | **William** | **Jolly** | 34 | Yaxley | Arson | **Sentence of death - Hanged Ipswich August 17th.** Details of trial: SC August 3rd; details of sentence: SC August 10th. Details of execution: SC August 24th. |
| Aug 2nd SC | 1834 | George | Moor | 22 | Framlingham | Rape | Death recorded.  Details SC August 2nd. Sentenced to be transported for life, but died before he could be sent. |
| Aug 2nd SC | 1834 | Daniel | Watson | 20 | Framlingham | Rape | Death recorded.  Details SC August 2nd. Transported for life to New South Wales in 1835. |
| Aug 2nd SC | 1834 | William | Jessop | 20 | Framlingham | Rape | Death recorded.  Details SC August 2nd. Transported for life to New South Wales in 1835. |
| Aug 2nd SC | 1834 | Thomas | Fletcher | 21 | Wyverstone | Burglary from Rector's house on a Sunday | Death recorded  Details of capture:  BP April 16th 1834. Transported for 14 years to Van Diemen's Land in 1834. |
| Aug 2nd SC | 1834 | James | Rushbrooke | 19 | Wyverstone | Burglary from Rector's house on a Sunday | Death recorded  Details of capture:  BP April 16th 1834 |
| Mar 28th SC | 1835 | **George** | **Pulham** | 22 | Lidgate | Arson | **Sentence of death - Hanged Bury April 8th.** Details of trial: SC March 28th; details of execution: SC April 11th. |
| Mar 28th SC | 1835 | William | Fairweather | 20 | Stoke by Nayland | Robbery with violence | Death recorded.  Transported for life to New South Wales in 1835. |

| Date of trial report | Year | Christian name | Surname | Age | Place offence committed | Crime | Outcome |
|---|---|---|---|---|---|---|---|
| Mar 28th SC | 1835 | Robert | Gillingwater | 20 | Stoke by Nayland | Robbery with violence | Death recorded. Transported for life to New South Wales in 1835. |
| Mar 28th SC | 1835 | Henry | Osborne | 23 | Little Wratting | Highway robbery | Death recorded |
| Mar 28th SC | 1835 | John | Chapman | 21 | Little Wratting | Highway robbery | Death recorded. Transported for life to New South Wales in 1835. |
| Mar 28th SC | 1835 | **Edward** | **Chalker** | 28 | Ipswich | Murder | **Sentence of death - Hanged Ipswich March 30th.** Details SC March 28th & April 4th |
| Aug 1st SC | 1835 | Phillip | Burrows | 22 | Dennington | Highway robbery | Death recorded  Details: SC August 1st |
| Aug 1st SC | 1835 | Isaac | Sheppard | 17 | Dennington | Highway robbery | Death recorded  Details: SC August 1st |
| Aug 1st SC | 1835 | Edward | Carter | 21 | Stoke by Nayland | Robbery | Death recorded  Details: SC August 1st. Transported for 14 years to New South Wales in 1835 |
| Aug 1st SC | 1835 | Elizabeth | Gooch | 45 | Farnham | Attempted murder | Death recorded.  Details: SC August 1st  Transported for life to New South Wales in 1835. |
| *Aug 1st SC* | *1835* | *Samuel* | *Brown* | *78* | *Woodbridge* | *Manslaughter* | *Death possibly not recorded.      Details: SC August 1st    Was tried for a murder committed 18 years earlier.  Transported for life to New South Wales in 1835.* |
| Mar 26th SC | 1836 | James | Burgess | 24 | Ipswich, St. Clements | Riotous Assembly (An attack on St. Clements Workhouse) | Death recorded.  Details: SC March 26th |
| Mar 26th SC | 1836 | Daniel | Folly | 52 (?) | Ipswich, St. Clements | Riotous Assembly (An attack on St. Clements Workhouse) | Death recorded.  Details: SC March 26th |
| Mar 26th SC | 1836 | Michael | Terry | 19 | Ipswich, St. Margaret | Riotous Assembly (An attack on St. Margarets Workhouse) | Death Recorded |

| Date of trial report | Year | Christian name | Surname | Age | Place offence committed | Crime | Outcome |
|---|---|---|---|---|---|---|---|
| Mar 26th SC | 1836 | Robert | Hurren | 19 | Ipswich, St. Margaret | Riotous Assembly (An attack on St. Margarets Workhouse) | Death Recorded |
| Mar 26th SC | 1836 | John | Simpson | 51 | Ipswich, St. Mary, Stoke | Attempted murder | Death recorded rather than sentenced as he shot at 'no vital part' of his victim. Details: SC March 26th |
| Mar 26th SC | 1836 | Henry | Gurney | 23 | Fornham | Attempted murder (shooting Dule of Norfolk's gamekeeper) | Death recorded  Details: SC March 26th  Transported for life to Van Diemen's Land in 1836 |
| Mar 26th SC | 1836 | Robert | Cook | 21 | Fornham | Attempted murder (shooting Dule of Norfolk's gamekeeper) | Death recorded  Details: SC March 26th  Reprieved and transported for 7 years to Van Diemen's Land in 1836 |
| Mar 26th SC | 1836 | James | Cotton | 34 | Reydon | House breaking | Death recorded  Details: SC March 26th  Transported for life to New South Wales in 1837 |
| Mar 26th SC | 1836 | Israel | Cotton | 31 | Reydon | House breaking | Death recorded  Details: SC March 26th  Sentenced to be transported for life but we found no evidence he ever  went. |
| Mar 26th SC | 1836 | Benjamin | Abbott | 17 | Eye | Highway robbery | Death recorded  Details: SC March 26th  Transported for 14 years to Van Diemen's Land in 1837 One of several Abbotts transported from this area. |
| Mar 26th SC | 1836 | Alfred | Marriott | 23 | Eye | Highway robbery | Death recorded  Details: SC March 26th  Transported for 14 years to Van Diemen's Land in 1836, dying soon after arriving there. |
| Mar 26th SC | 1836 | William | Tye | 20 | Stonham | Stealing liquors | Death recorded  Details: SC March 26th  Transported for life to Van Diemen's Land in 1836 |

| Date of trial report | Year | Christian name | Surname | Age | Place offence committed | Crime | Outcome |
|---|---|---|---|---|---|---|---|
| Mar 26th SC | 1836 | John | Hempstead | 27 | Great Finborough | Burglary | Death recorded Details: SC March 26th Transported for life to Van Diemen's Land in 1836 |
| Mar 26th SC | 1836 | James | Tampion | 50 | Great Finborough | Burglary | Death recorded Details: SC March 26th Transported for life to Van Diemen's Land in 1836 |
| Mar 26th SC | 1836 | William | Tampion | 22 | Great Finborough | Burglary | Death recorded Details: SC March 26th Transported for life to Van Diemen's Land in 1836 |
| Apr 1st SC | 1837 | Charles | Diaper or Draper | 21 | Needham Market | Highway robbery | Death recorded Details: SC April 1st Reprieved and sentenced to transportation, but we can find no evidence he ever went |
| Apr 1st SC | 1837 | Samuel | Squirrel | 20 | Needham Market | Highway robbery | Death recorded Details: SC April 1st Transported to Van Diemen's Land in 1837 |
| Apr 1st SC | 1837 | Charles | Ablitt | 17 | Ipswich | Burglary | Death recorded Details: SC April 1st |
| Apr 1st SC | 1837 | Samuel | Arnold | 16 | Bury St. Edmunds | Robbery with violence | Death recorded Details: SC April 1st |
| Apr 1st SC | 1837 | Jonathan | Woollard Jun. | | Kersey | Blackmail | Death recorded Details: SC April 1st Sentence commuted to transportation for 7 years. Transported to New South Wales in 1837 |
| July 29th SC | 1837 | George | Baker | 27 | Rickinghall | Highway robbery | Death recorded Details: SC July 29th Transported for 7 years to Van Diemen's Land in 1838 |
| July 29th SC | 1837 | James | Pannifer | 16 | | Bestiality (an unnatural crime) | Death recorded Transported to New South Wales for life in 1837 |

| Date of trial report | Year | Christian name | Surname | Age | Place offence committed | Crime | Outcome |
|---|---|---|---|---|---|---|---|
| Apr 4th SC | 1840 | William | Simpson | 45 | Beccles | Rape of a child of 10 | Death possibly recorded; sentence commuted to one of transportation, though it is unlikely he ever went. Details: SC April 4th |
| Apr 3rd SC | 1841 | Henry | Foster | 20 | Shimpling | Highway robbery; cutting and maiming his victim | Death possibly recorded. Details: SC April 3rd  Sentence commuted and transported for life to Van Diemen's Land in 1841 |
| Apr 3rd SC | 1841 | Charles | Fenn | 17 | Shimpling | Highway robbery; cutting and maiming his victim | Death possibly recorded. Details: SC April 3rd  Sentence commuted and transported for life to Van Diemen's Land in 1841 |
| Apr 1st SC | 1843 | George | Manning | 20 | Bacton | Burglary with menaces | Death recorded.  Details: SC April 1st  Sentence commuted - Transported for life to New South Wales in 1843 |
| Apr 1st SC | 1843 | Thomas | Rampling | 35 | Bacton | Burglary with menaces | Death recorded.  Details: SC April 1st  Listed for transportation for 14 years |
| Apr 1st SC | 1843 | Charles | Smith | 23 | Hadleigh | Manslaughter | Death possibly recorded - charge reduced from the original one of murder.  Details: SC April 1st |
| Apr 1st SC | 1843 | Charles | Cole | 28 | Ipswich | Manslaughter | Death possibly recorded - charge reduced from the original one of murder.  Details: SC April 1st |
| Dec 14th SC | 1844 | Mary | Sheming | 51 | Martlesham | Murder of her granddaughter | **Sentence of death - Hanged Ipswich January 11th 1845** after a respite.  Details: SC December 14th; execution details - SC January 18th; further info + poem - SC January 25th   Her brother James Green had been transported in 1836. |

| Date of trial report | Year | Christian name | Surname | Age | Place offence committed | Crime | Outcome |
|---|---|---|---|---|---|---|---|
| Dec 21st SC | 1844 | **William** | **Howell** | 28 | **Gisleham** | Shooting of Police Constable | **Sentence of death respited until January 25th 1845 when he was hanged at Ipswich 25th 1845. Details: SC December 21st 1844, SC January 25th 1845, SC February 1st 1845** |
| Dec 21st SC | 1844 | Walter | Howell | 21 | Gisleham | Shooting of Police Constable | Sentence of death respited until January 25th when he was reprieved. Transported for life to Norfolk Island in 1845 |
| Dec 21st SC | 1844 | Israel | Shipley | 28 | Gisleham | Shooting of Police Constable | Sentence of death respited until January 25th when he was reprieved. Transported for life to Van Diemen's Land in 1846 |
| *Apr 5th SC* | *1845* | *William* | *Tibbenham* | *32* | *Wantisden* | *Murder of his wife (improper use of a firearm whilst drunk)* | *Jury were prepared to find him guilty of murder, but on direction of the judge, reduced conviction to manslaughter. Probably death not recorded - One year hard labour. Details: SC April 5th* |
| Aug 2nd SC | 1845 | John | Catchpole | 47 | Ipswich | Assault on his wife | Death recorded but reprieved and transported for 15 years to Van Diemen's Land in 1846. Details: SC August 2nd |
| *Mar 21st SC* | *1846* | *Thomas* | *Dykes* | *27* | *Buxhall* | *Stabbed a police constable* | *Murder reduced to manslaughter as the victim had taken some time to die. Death probably not recorded. Transported for life to Van Diemen's Land in 1846. Details: SC March 21st* |

| Date of trial report | Year | Christian name | Surname | Age | Place offence committed | Crime | Outcome |
|---|---|---|---|---|---|---|---|
| Apr 3rd SC | 1847 | Catherine | Foster | 18 | Acton | Murder of her husband | **Hanged at Bury St. Edmunds April 17th.** Details of case: SC April 3rd. Details of execution & questions asked in House of Lords: SC April 24th |
| July 31st SC | 1847 | George | Barker | 29 | Ipswich St. Margaret's | Murder, later reduced to manslaughter | Death probably not recorded. Finally sentenced to transportation for 20 years, but we found no evidence he ever went. |
| Apr 1st SC | 1848 | Robert | Welham | 37 | Bradfield Combust | Murderous assault & robbery | Death recorded. Details: SC April 1st |
| Apr 12th SC | 1851 | Maria | Clarke | 22 | Wingfield | Murder of her child | Sentence of death. Details: SC April 12th. Respited as Calcraft, the only executioner in the kingdom was busy elsewhere. (SC April 19th) A plea for further respite (SC April 19th) appears to have been upheld and a reprieve obtained. |
| Apr 5th SC | 1851 | George | Carnt (or Gant) | 23 | Lawshall | Murder by drowning | **Sentence of death. Hanged at Bury St. Edmunds April 22nd 1851.** Details: SC April 5th, SC April 26th. |
| Apr 12th SC (case deferred as she had only just been arrested) Aug 9th SC | 1851 | Mary | Cage | 40 | Stonham Aspal | Poisoned her husband | **Sentence of death. Hanged at Ipswich August 19th.** Details: SC April 5th, SC August 9th, SC August 23rd |

| Date of trial report | Year | Christian name | Surname | Age | Place offence committed | Crime | Outcome |
|---|---|---|---|---|---|---|---|
| Mar 27th SC | 1852 | John | Mickleburgh | 41 | Thrandeston | Murder of Mary Baker, his servant & mistress | Sentence of death. Details: SC March 20th Plea for clemency submitted to Home Secretary (SC: April 3rd) Reprieved as he was described as suffering from a 'diseased intellect' (SC April 10th) |
| Mar 27th SC | 1852 | William | Robinson | 80 | Great Thurlow | Poisoning by arsenic of Ann Cornell | Sentence of death. Details: SC March 20th Respite of execution owing to his age (SC April 10th) |
| Mar 27th SC | 1852 | William | Baldry | 38 | Preston | Attempting to murder his wife with poison | Sentence of death. Details: SC March 20th. Respite of execution till May 8th (SC April 3rd) followed by further respite. |
| July 30th SC (supplement) | 1853 | William | Flack | 18 | Bacton | Murder of Maria Steggles | Sentence of death. Details of examination: SC June 11th; trial and awaiting execution: SC July 30th, August 6th, August 13th. Hanged at Ipswich: August 17th (SC August 20th) |
| Aug 5th SC (supplement) | 1854 | Emma | Moyse | 18 | Charsfield | Arson - set fire to her master's house | Death recorded, reduced to 4 years penal servitude. Details: SC August 5th |
| Aug 4th SC (supplement) | 1855 | John | Newton | | Brandon | An unnatural offence | Sentence of death, recommending his life be spared. Transported for life to Western Australia in 1857 |
| Mar 29th SC | 1856 | George | French | 73 | Denham | An unnatural offence | Death recorded, recommending a commutation of sentence. |
| Mar 29th SC | 1856 | Emma | Mussett | 30 | Nayland | Murder of her child | Sentence of death. Details: SC March 29th. Reprieved (SC: April 5th) |
| Jul 29th SC | 1856 | John | Baker | 16 | Boxford | An unnatural offence | Death recorded. Transported for 15 years to Western Australia in 1857 |

| Date of trial report | Year | Christian name | Surname | Age | Place offence committed | Crime | Outcome |
|---|---|---|---|---|---|---|---|
| May 27th SC | 1858 | Emma | Groom | 24 | Oakley | Murder of her child | Sentence of death. Details: SC March 27th (trial), respite reported SC April 3rd, followed by a reprieve. |
| July 31st SC | 1858 | **Ebeneezer** | **Cherrington** | 27 | Ipswich St. Mary Elm | Murder of Susan Studd | **Sentence of death.** Details: SC July 31st. Suggestion of possible reprieve SC: August 7th. **Executed at Ipswich on August 17th.** Details and editorial: SC August 21st |
| Apr 2nd SC (supplement) | 1859 | Jonathan | Buckle | 18 | Bury St. Edmunds | An unnatural offence | Death recorded but the final sentence was to be 'a long period of penal servitude.' |
| Mar 28th SC | 1863 | **John** | **Ducker** | 63 | Halesworth | Murder of Ebenezer Tye, a policeman | **Sentence of death.** Details: SC March 28th (trial) **Executed at Ipswich on Tuesday 14th April.** Details: SC April 18th. |
| Aug 7th BP | 1866 | Hannah | Colthorpe | 37 | Sproughton | Murder of a child | Sentence of death, but a strong recommendation for mercy. Details: BP August 7th. Respite reported BP August 14th. Life imprisonment |
| Mar 26th BFP (supplement) | 1870 | James | Rutterford | 27 | Eriswell | Murder of a gamekeeper | Sentence of death Details: BFP March 26th/April 9th Reprieved as it was believed he could not be safely hanged due to a malformation of his neck. Attempted gaol escape (Diss Express March 4th 1870) |
| Apr 8th BFP | 1876 | Elizabeth | Swatman | 45 | Belton | Murder | Sentence of death. Details: BFP April 8th. Described as of low intellect and apparently reprieved |

| Date of trial report | Year | Christian name | Surname | Age | Place offence committed | Crime | Outcome |
|---|---|---|---|---|---|---|---|
| Aug 4th BFP | 1877 | Mary Jane | Brown | 27 | Lowestoft | Murder of her 3 children | Sentence of death. Details: BFP August 4th. Petition for mercy (BFP August 11th) Confession (BFP August 18th) Respite of sentence (BFP August 25th) Her husband Samuel was acquitted of murder. |
| Nov 15th BFP | 1879 | Henry | **Bedingfield** | 46 | Ipswich | Murder + attempted suicide | **Sentence of death.** Details: BFP November 15th/22nd. Petition for mercy (BFP November 29th) **Hanged at Ipswich on December 3rd** - reported in BFP/SC December 6th. |
| Feb 12th SC | 1881 | Joseph | Wilson | 21 | Ipswich | Murder - drowned a woman in Ipswich dock | Sentence of death. Details: SC February 12th. Recommendation to mercy (SC February 19th) Reprieved (SC February 26th) |
| Oct 27th SC | 1883 | **Thomas Lyons** | **Day** | 31 | Ipswich | Murder | **Sentence of death.** Details: SC October 27th & November 10th. **Hanged at Ipswich on November 13th.** See letter to SC November 17th. |
| Nov 15th SC | 1884 | Edna | Carter | 21 | Wrentham | Murder of her child | Sentence of death. Details: SC November 15th Respited (SC November 22nd) & finally reprieved. |
| Feb 6th BFP | 1886 | **George** | **Saunders** | 29 | Lowestoft | Murder of his wife | **Sentence of death.** Details: BFP February 6th. **Executed at Ipswich on February 16th.** Report: BFP February 20th Report detailing failure of application for remission of sentence: Norfolk Mail: February 16th |

| Date of trial report | Year | Christian name | Surname | Age | Place offence committed | Crime | Outcome |
|---|---|---|---|---|---|---|---|
| Dec 10th SC | 1892 | John James | McCabe | 25 | Ipswich | Murder | Sentence of death; recommended mercy. Details: SC December 10th  Respite reported SC December 17th.  Commuted to life imprisonment  SC December 24th |
| June 17th SC | 1899 | Ada | Brown | 20 | Stowmarket | Murder of her daughter | Sentence of death  Details SC June 17th  Reprieve reported in Stowmarket Courier June 22nd.  She was visited by the Bishop of Norwich shortly before her sentence was commuted to life imprisonment |
| Nov 3rd SC | 1899 | George | Nunn | 18 | Wortham | Murder | **Sentence of death  Details SC November 3rd.  Taken by train to be executed at Ipswich on November 21st.**  Report with picture SC November 24th |
| Nov 9th SC | 1900 | Ellis | Backler | 49 | Haverhill | Murder of his common-law wife and two of their children | Sentence of death  Details SC November 9th (in 2 parts)  Reprieve on the grounds of insanity reported  SC November 23rd. |